双语阅读世界经典童话

（英汉对照）

佩罗童话

The Fairy Tales of Charles Perrault

【法】夏尔·佩罗 著
【爱尔兰】哈利·克拉克 绘
丁大琴 刘慧 译

北京师范大学出版集团
BEIJING NORMAL UNIVERSITY PUBLISHING GROUP
安徽大学出版社

图书在版编目(CIP)数据

佩罗童话:英汉对照/(法)夏尔·佩罗著;丁大琴,刘慧译. —合肥:安徽大学出版社,2023.3

(双语阅读世界经典童话)

ISBN 978-7-5664-2559-1

Ⅰ.①佩… Ⅱ.①夏… ②丁… ③刘… Ⅲ.①英语—汉语—对照读物②童话—法国—近代 Ⅳ.①H319.4:I

中国版本图书馆 CIP 数据核字(2023)第 000699 号

佩罗童话(英汉对照)

[法]夏尔·佩罗 著
丁大琴 刘 慧 译

出版发行:	北京师范大学出版集团
	安 徽 大 学 出 版 社
	(安徽省合肥市肥西路3号 邮编230039)
	www.bnupg.com
	www.ahupress.com.cn
印 刷:	安徽利民印务有限公司
经 销:	全国新华书店
开 本:	787 mm×1092 mm 1/16
印 张:	7.25
字 数:	218 千字
版 次:	2023 年 3 月第 1 版
印 次:	2023 年 3 月第 1 次印刷
定 价:	29.90 元

ISBN 978-7-5664-2559-1

策划编辑:李 梅 葛灵知	装帧设计:李 军
责任编辑:高婷婷	美术编辑:李 军
责任校对:李 雪	责任印制:赵明炎

版权所有　侵权必究

反盗版、侵权举报电话:0551—65106311
外埠邮购电话:0551—65107716
本书如有印装质量问题,请与印制管理部联系调换。
印制管理部电话:0551—65106311

序 言

童话是青少年成长成才、身心健康发展的摇篮。优秀的童话不仅能够愉悦孩子的心情，丰富孩子的想象力，还能提升孩子的应变能力和为人处事能力，向其传递正确的价值观、人生观和世界观，真正将寓教于乐落到实处。优秀的童话经过时间的洗涤，在薪火相传中延续其文化内涵和精神价值，成为孩子不可或缺的精神食粮，陶冶他们的情操。

17世纪末，"法国儿童文学之父"夏尔·佩罗从民间传说中寻找文学创作的源泉，汲取灵感，收集并整理了大量的故事，将其汇编成书。本书中的童话虽距今三百多年，但依旧深得人心，洋溢着青春的活力，其根本原因在于佩罗能够借助简洁朴素的语言和生动形象的故事来歌颂真善美，抨击假恶丑，并赞扬了反抗压迫和争取自由的精神。这些精神价值都是人们对美好生活的向往和追求，永不过时。

为了帮助国内青少年更好地了解童话中所蕴含的精神价值，从中汲取精神营养，本书收录了佩罗富含哲理的经典童话集《鹅妈妈的故事》中的一些脍炙人口的经典佳作，例如《灰姑娘》《小红帽》《林中睡美人》《小拇指》《蓝胡子》《穿靴子的猫》等。在这些童话中，有的反映真实的社会面貌，有的蕴含严肃的人生准则，给人以启迪。譬如，《小红帽》揭露了封建统治者的昏庸残暴；《灰姑娘》歌颂了劳动人民的勤劳、善良和正直；《小拇指》赞扬了小主人翁巧妙化解危机的的聪明睿智。这些童话不仅能够影响孩子人格的塑造，还能教会他们勇敢面对困难、机智应对危机。

  与此同时，为了打造纯英文的阅读环境，本书在编排上采用"先中后英"的模式，力求借助青少年对童话的热爱，激发其英语学习兴趣，提升双语阅读能力，真正贯彻落实寓教于乐的理念。因此，在翻译过程中，译者在尽量还原故事和内涵的基础上，力求语言简洁朴素、故事生动有趣，让青少年在阅读经典童话中体会阅读的乐趣。对于文中出现的一些特殊词汇，译者在充分考虑青少年读者的知识水平的基础上，采取加注的形式进行解释，帮助其理解。

  本书致力于让青少年阅读世界优秀童话，汲取世界之精华，帮助孩子健康成长。本书难免有不足之处，欢迎广大读者批评指正，以期再版重印时加以修订完善。

丁大琴
2023 年 3 月

目录 CONTENTS

小红帽 / 1

Little Red Riding Hood / 4

仙女 / 7

The Fairy / 10

蓝胡子 / 13

Blue Beard / 19

林中睡美人 / 25

The Sleeping Beauty in the Wood / 35

穿靴子的猫 / 45

The Master Cat or Puss in Boots / 50

灰姑娘 / 55

Cinderilla or the Little Glass Slipper / 62

小凤头里凯 / 69

Riquet with the Tuft / 76

小拇指 / 83

Little Thumb / 93

荒谬的愿望 / 103

The Ridiculous Wishes / 107

小红帽

从前，有个村子里住着一位小女孩，美若天仙，无人能及。妈妈非常疼爱她，外婆对她更是宠爱有加。外婆心地善良，给小女孩织了一顶小小的红帽子；小女孩戴上后显得格外漂亮。从那以后，人人都唤她"小红帽"了。

一天，妈妈做了一些糕饼，就对小红帽说："宝贝，我听说外婆生病了，很严重。你拿上这块糕饼，还有小罐黄油，去看看外婆怎么样了。"

听了妈妈的话，小红帽立即出发，去看望住在隔壁村的外婆。就在穿过一片树林时，她遇见了一只大灰狼。大灰狼很想吃掉小红帽，但他还不敢这么做，因为这个时候树林附近还有一些砍柴的樵夫。

于是，大灰狼就问小红帽要去哪儿。可怜的小红帽哪里知道停下来同大灰狼讲话有多么危险，于是就回答道："我要去看望外婆，妈妈给她准备了一块糕饼，还有一小罐黄油呢。"

大灰狼问道："她家离这儿远吗？"

"嗯，很远，"小红帽回答道，"你看那边有个磨坊。她就住在那个磨坊后面，村子前头的第一家。"

"正好，"大灰狼说道，"我也打算去看望她。我走这条路，你走那条路，看看我们俩谁先到。"

随后，大灰狼便顺着最近的路拼命向前跑去。小红帽则沿着那条最远的路走去。这一路上她边走边玩，一会儿捡些坚果，一会儿追逐蝴蝶，一会儿摘些小野花，并做成花环。不一会儿，大灰狼就来到了外婆家门口，轻轻地叩起门来。

"谁呀？"

"您的宝贝孙女，小红帽，"大灰狼模仿小红帽的声音答道，"我给您带来了妈妈做的一块糕饼和一小罐黄油。"

善良的外婆生病了，躺在床上，大声说道："你拉一下绳子，门栓就掉下来了。"

大灰狼拉了一下绳子，门就打开了。大灰狼进屋后，立马扑向善良的外婆，一下子就把外婆吞进了肚子，因为他已经超过三天没有吃东西了。随后，大灰狼拴上门，躺在外婆的床上，等着即将赶到的小红帽前来敲门。

"谁呀？"

起初，小红帽听到大灰狼的大嗓门，害怕极了。然而，一想到外婆可能是因为生病，所以声音哑了，才会这样，小红帽就回答道："外婆，我是您的宝贝孙女，小红帽呀！我给您带来了妈妈做的一块糕饼和一小罐黄油呢。"

大灰狼尽可能让声音听起来温柔一点，对小红帽说道："你拉一下绳子，门栓就掉下来了。"

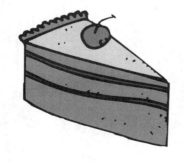

小红帽拉了一下绳子，门果然就开了。大灰狼一看见小红帽来了，便用被子遮住自己说："你先把糕饼和小罐黄油放到面包箱里，然后过来陪我躺会儿。"

放好糕饼和小罐黄油，小红帽就脱

了衣服，爬到外婆的床上，却意外发现穿着睡衣的外婆很是奇怪，就问道："外婆，你的胳膊怎么这么长呀？"

"这样才更方便抱你呢，宝贝。"

"外婆，你的腿怎么这么长呀！"

"这样才能跑得更快呀，孩子。"

"外婆，你的耳朵怎么这么大呀！"

"这样才能听得更清楚嘛，孩子。"

"外婆，那你的眼睛怎么这么大呀！"

"这样才能看得更清楚啊，孩子。"

"外婆，那你的牙齿怎么这么大呀！"

"当然是为了吃掉你。"

说完这些话，这只邪恶的大灰狼就扑向可怜的小红帽，把她吃掉了。

Little Red Riding Hood

Once upon a time, there lived in a certain village, a little country girl, the prettiest creature was ever seen. Her mother was excessively fond of her; and her grandmother doted on her much more. This good woman got made for her a little red riding hood, which became the girl so extremely well that everybody called her Little Red Riding Hood.

One day, her mother, having made some girdle-cakes, said to her, "Go, my dear, and see how your grandmamma does, for I hear she has been very ill, carry her a girdle-cake, and this little pot of butter."

Little Red Riding Hood set out immediately to go to her grandmother, who lived in another village. As she was going through the wood, she met with Gaffer Wolf, who had a very great mind to eat her up, but he dared not, because of some faggot-makers hard by in the forest.

He asked her whither she was going. The poor child, who did not know that it was dangerous to stay and hear a wolf talk, said to him, "I am going to see my grandmamma, and carry her a girdle-cake, and a little pot of butter, from my mamma."

"Does she live far off?" said the wolf.

"Oh! Yes," answered Little Red Riding Hood, "it is beyond that mill you see there, at the first house in the village."

"Well," said the wolf, "and I'll go and see her too. I'll go this way, and you go that, and we shall see who will be there soonest."

The wolf began to run as fast as he could, taking the nearest way; and the little girl went by that farthest about, diverting herself in gathering nuts, running after butterflies, and making nosegays of such little flowers as she met with. The wolf was not long before he got to the old woman's house: he knocked at the door, tap, tap.

"Who's there?"

"Your grandchild, Little Red Riding Hood," replied the wolf, counterfeiting her voice, "who has brought you a girdle-cake, and a little pot of butter, sent you by Mamma."

The good grandmother, who was in bed, because she found herself somewhat ill, cried out, "Pull the string, and the bolt will fall."

The wolf pulled the string, and the door opened, and then presently he fell upon the good woman, and ate her up in a moment; for it was above three days that he had not touched a bit. He then shut the door, and went into the grandmother's bed, expecting Little Red Riding Hood, who came some time afterwards, and knocked at the door, tap, tap.

"Who's there?"

Little Red Riding Hood, hearing the big voice of the wolf, was at first afraid; but believing her grandmother had got a cold, and was hoarse, answered, "It is your grandchild, Little Red Riding Hood, who has brought you a girdle-cake, and a little pot of butter, Mamma sends you."

The wolf cried out to her, softening his voice as much as he could, "Pull the string, and the bolt will fall."

Little Red Riding Hood pulled the string, and the door opened. The wolf seeing her come in, said to her, hiding himself under the bedclothes, "Put the cake, and the little pot of butter upon the bread-bin, and come and lie down with me."

Little Red Riding Hood undressed herself, and went into bed; where, being greatly amazed to see how her grandmother looked in her night-clothes, she said to her, "Grandmamma, what great arms you have got!"

"That is the better to hug you, my dear."

"Grandmamma, what great legs you have got!"

"That is to run the better, my child."

"Grandmamma, what great ears you have got!"

"That is to hear the better, my child."

"Grandmamma, what great eyes you have got!"

"It is to see the better, my child."

"Grandmamma, what great teeth you have got!"

"That is to eat you up."

And, saying these words, this wicked wolf fell upon poor Little Red Riding Hood, and ate her all up.

仙女

从前,有一个寡妇,养育了两个女儿。大女儿无论是外貌还是性情,都和她很像,谁见了大女儿都会不由自主地想起这位寡妇。然而,这母女俩又都非常傲慢,不招人喜欢,因此没有人愿意和她们打交道。但是小女儿简直就是父亲的缩小版,不仅举止文雅,性格温柔,更是绝色美人。人们对自己外貌存在天生的喜爱感,所以寡妇非常宠爱大女儿,厌恶小女儿。她不仅让小女儿在厨房吃饭,还总是让她干活。

除此之外,可怜的小女儿每天都要去离家超过两千四百米的泉水边打两趟水,并带着盛满水的水罐回家。一天,小女儿正在泉水边打水时,一位可怜的妇人朝她走来,求她给点水喝。

"噢,好哇,我就来。"美丽的小女儿一边说着,一边马上把水罐洗干净,从泉水最清澈的地方舀出一点水,递给老妇人。而且,老妇人喝水的时候,小女儿为了她喝水方便就一直举着水罐。

心地善良的老妇人喝完水,对小女儿说:"丫头,你人长得漂亮,心地也善良,待人还温和,我很想送你一件礼物。"(原来这个老妇人是仙女,她故意化作可怜的乡下妇人,就是想试探试探这个小女孩到底有多善良文雅。)"我这就送你一件礼物,"仙女继续说道,"有了它,只要你张嘴说话,就会有鲜花或者珠宝从你嘴里冒出来。"

漂亮的小女儿一回到家,妈妈就开始斥责她,嫌弃她回来晚了。

"对不起,妈妈,"可怜的小女儿说道,"我应该快点回来的。"就在小女儿说这些话的时候,她的嘴里就吐出来两朵玫瑰、两粒珍珠,还有两颗钻石。

"我看到了什么?"妈妈震惊地说道,"我竟然看到珍珠和钻石从你嘴里冒出来!发生了什么,我的女儿?"(这可是她第一次叫小女儿为"女儿"。)

可怜的小女儿把刚才发生的一切都告诉了妈妈,在这期间又有大量钻石从她嘴里冒了出来。

"天哪,"妈妈喊道,"我一定要让大女儿到那边去看看。芬妮,快点过来,快看看你妹妹一张嘴说话就吐出了什么来。亲爱的,你要是拥有了这一本领,那该多好啊!你现在快去泉边打水,如果有一个可怜的妇人向你要水喝,你一定要恭恭敬敬地递给她。"

"我去打水?"傲慢无礼的大女儿说道,"那可真是一道靓丽的风景!"

"必须去,"妈妈说道,"现在就去。"

最后大女儿拿着家里最好的银罐去了,但是一路上抱怨个不停。

大女儿刚到泉水边,就看见一位衣着华丽的贵族小姐从小树林里走过来,向自己要水喝。你们一定猜到了,这就是刚才向小女儿讨水喝的仙女,不过她这次故意化为一位公主的模样,来试探这个大女儿到底有多粗鲁无礼。

"难道我来这儿,"傲慢无礼的大女儿戏谑道,"就是专门给你送水的嘛?这个银罐儿,可是专门拿来给一个老妇人喝水用的。不过,你想喝就喝吧。"

"真是太没礼貌了,"仙女面无表情地回答道,"既然你如此无礼,冷酷无情,我也送你一件礼物吧,你只要开口说话,就会有蛇和癞蛤蟆从你嘴里爬出来。"

妈妈一看见大女儿回来了，就向她喊道："怎么样了，女儿？"

"什么呀，妈妈？"粗鲁的大女儿回答道，然后就有两条毒蛇和两只癞蛤蟆从她嘴里爬了出来。

"哦，天啦！"妈妈大叫道，"我看见了什么！这一切都是你那歹毒的妹妹造成的，我一定要找她算账。"说着，妈妈立即冲向小女儿，把她暴打一顿。可怜的小女儿逃了出来，躲到了离家不远的小树林里。

此时，国王的儿子刚打完猎，在回宫的路上遇见了小女儿，见她如此漂亮，就上前问她为何独自待在这儿，又因何事而流泪。

"唉，先生，我被妈妈赶出来了。"

其间，五六颗珍珠和许多钻石从小女儿的嘴里冒了出来。看到这一幕，王子非常好奇，迫切想要知道为什么会这样。于是，小女儿就把事情的经过都告诉了王子。因此，王子爱上了小女儿，心想这礼物可比其他女孩的嫁妆都要珍贵，然后就带她来到了国王的宫殿，在那里与她成了亲。

至于姐姐，因为太不招人喜欢，被妈妈赶了出去。后来，这个可怜的大女儿就长期在外流浪，没有人愿意收留她，最后死在了小树林的一个角落里。

The Fairy

There was, once upon a time, a widow, who had two daughters. The eldest was so much like her in the face and humor, that whoever looked upon the daughter saw the mother. They were both so disagreeable, and so proud that there was no living with them. The youngest, who was the very picture of her father, for courtesy and sweetness of temper, was withal one of the most beautiful girls ever seen. As people naturally love their own likeness, this mother even doted on her eldest daughter, and at the same time had a horrible aversion for the youngest. She made her eat in the kitchen, and work continually.

Among other things, this poor child was forced twice a day to draw water above a mile and a half off the house, and bring home a pitcher full of it. One day, as she was at this fountain, there came to her a poor woman, who begged of her to let her drink.

"O, yes, with all my heart, Goody," said this pretty maid; and rinsing immediately the pitcher, she took up some water from the clearest place of the fountain, and gave it to her, holding up the pitcher all the while, that she might drink the easier.

The good woman having drank, said to her, "You are so very pretty, my dear, so good and so mannerly, that I cannot help giving you a gift." (For this was a fairy, who had taken the form of a poor country-woman, to see how far the civility and good manners of this pretty girl would go.) "I will give you a gift," continued the fairy, "that at every word you speak, there shall come out of your mouth either a flower, or a jewel."

When this pretty girl came home, her mother scolded at her for staying so long at the fountain.

"I beg your pardon, Mamma," said the poor girl, "for not making more haste." And in speaking these words, there came out of her mouth two roses, two pearls, and two diamonds.

"What is this I see?" said her mother quite astonished. "I think I see pearls and diamonds come out of the girl's mouth! How happens this, child?" (This was the first time she ever called her child.)

The poor creature told her frankly all the matter, not without dropping out infinite numbers of diamonds.

"In good faith," cried the mother, "I must send my child thither. Come hither, Fanny, look what comes out of your sister's mouth when she speaks. Wouldn't you be glad, my dear, to have the same gift given to you? You has nothing else to do but go and draw water out of the fountain, and when a certain poor woman asks you to let her drink, give it to her very civilly."

"It would be a very fine sight indeed," said this ill-bred minx, "to see me go draw water!"

"You shall go," said the mother, "and this minute."

So away she went, but grumbling all the way, taking with her the best silver tankard in the house.

She was no sooner at the fountain, than she saw coming out of the wood a lady most gloriously dressed, who came up to her, and asked to drink. This was, you must know, the very fairy who appeared to her sister, but had now taken the air and dress of a princess, to see how far this girl's rudeness would go.

"Do I come hither," said the proud, saucy slut, "to serve you with water, pray? I suppose the silver tankard was brought purely for your ladyship, was it? However, you may drink out of it, if you have a fancy."

"You are not over and above mannerly," answered the fairy, without putting herself in a passion. "Well then, since you have so little breeding, and are so disobliging, I give you a gift that at every word you speak there shall come out of your mouth a snake or a toad."

So soon as her mother saw her coming, she cried out, "Well, daughter?"

"Well, mother?" answered the pert hussy, throwing out of her mouth two vipers and two toads.

"O mercy!" cried the mother. "What is it I see! O, it is that wretch her sister who has occasioned all this; but she shall pay for it." And immediately she ran to beat her. The poor child fled away from her and went to hide herself in the forest, not far from thence.

The king's son, then on his return from hunting, met her, and seeing her so very pretty, asked her what she did there alone, and why she cried.

"Alas! Sir, my mamma has turned me out of doors."

The king's son, who saw five or six pearls, and as many diamonds, come out of her mouth, desired her to tell him how that happened. She thereupon told him the whole story; and so the king's son fell in love with her; and, considering with himself that such a gift was worth more than any marriage-portion whatsoever in another, conducted her to the palace of the king his father, and there married her.

As for her sister, she made herself so much hated that her own mother turned her off; and the miserable wretch, having wandered about a good while without finding anybody to take her in, went to a corner in the wood and there died.

蓝胡子

从前，有一个男子拥有许多漂亮的房子，城里和乡下都有，还有各式各样的金银餐具、刺绣的家具以及镀金的马车。但不幸的是，这个男子长着蓝色的胡子。这让他看起来既吓人又丑陋，以致妇女和姑娘们都躲他躲得远远的。

在他隔壁住着一位高贵优雅的夫人及其两个倾国倾城的女儿。蓝胡子就想着要是能娶她俩中的一人为妻就好了，至于到底娶哪一个，就要看夫人的意愿了。然而两个女儿都不喜欢他，互相劝说对方喜欢他，但谁都不愿意嫁给一个有着蓝胡子的男子。不过最令她们感到厌恶和反感的是，蓝胡子之前已经娶过好几任妻子了，而且全离奇失踪了，没有人知道她们的下落。

蓝胡子为了获得两姐妹的好感，就邀请她们及其母亲、三四个女性好友和周围几个年轻人前往他乡下的房子做客，并在那儿待了整整一周。在乡下，他们每天不是聚会、狩猎、钓鱼，就是跳舞、饮宴，享受着这里的欢声笑语。在这里，晚上根本没人睡觉，大家都是通宵达旦地玩耍。总之，一切都非常顺利，小女儿甚至开始认为房子的主人——蓝胡子的胡子也没有那么丑陋、吓人了，反而觉得他是一个既强大又文雅的绅士。所以等他们一回到家，两人就举办了婚礼。

大约一个月后，蓝胡子告诉妻子，

自己因为一些非常重要的事情，不得不到乡下去一趟，至少要六个星期才能回来。蓝胡子还说到，他不在的这段时间，妻子可以呼朋唤友，带他们去乡下游玩，只要妻子高兴，无论去哪儿都可宴饮作乐。

"这些，"他还说，"是家中两大藏衣室的钥匙，里面放的都是我最值钱的家具；这些钥匙是用来开柜子的，柜子里放着一些平时不怎么用的金银餐具；这些钥匙是用来开我的保险箱的，里面都是些金银财宝；这些钥匙是用来开珠宝盒的；这一把是万能钥匙，能打开所有房间的门；这儿还有这把小钥匙用来开地下室走廊尽头的仓库。你可以打开这里所有的房间，自由进出其中的任意一间，但唯独这间仓库不可以。我现在告诉你，你绝不可以进去；如果你碰巧打开了这间仓库，我一定会大发雷霆。"

妻子保证一定会严格遵守蓝胡子的嘱咐。随后蓝胡子拥抱妻子，就走上马车出发了。

妻子的邻居和好朋友都没有等这位新婚女士前来邀请自己，就急匆匆赶了过去，因为她们已经迫不及待地想要好好欣赏一下她家中这些昂贵的家具了，毕竟之前因为害怕蓝胡子，所以她们都不敢在他在家的时候过来。她们迅速看遍了所有卧室、书房和藏衣室，只见一个比一个漂亮，一个比一个华丽。

后来，他们走进了两个大房间，里面都是一些最华丽、最昂贵的家具。朋友们见了这些壁毯、床、沙发、橱柜、高台、桌子以及从头照到脚的穿衣镜后都赞叹不已。这些家具有的镶着玻璃边框，有的镶着银边框，还有的镶着镀金边框，她们可从没见过这么精美而又华丽的家具，于是她们不停地称赞妻子，羡慕她真是太幸福了。不过，此时此刻妻子对这些富丽堂皇的东西根本不感兴趣，因为她早已迫不及待地想要打开地下室的仓库了。在强烈的好奇心驱使下，妻子根本顾不上礼节，丢下朋友就独自离开了。然后她就沿着后面的一个小楼梯下去，其间由于太过匆忙她有两三次都差点折断脖子。

妻子来到仓库门口，想起了丈夫对她的叮嘱，心想如果违背丈夫的禁令，很有可能会给自己带来不幸，就在门口踌躇了一会；但她的好奇心太过强烈了，根本无法战胜理智。于是她便拿出了那把小钥匙，颤颤巍巍地打开门，刚开始由于仓库的窗户紧闭着，她根本看不清里面的东西，过了一会，她才发现地板上满是凝固的血迹，并排靠在墙边的几个女人的尸体倒映其中。这些可都是蓝胡子的前妻，原来她们都被蓝胡子给杀害了。看到这儿，她害怕得要命，连从锁眼里拔出的那把钥匙也猛地从手中掉了下来。

之后，她回过神来，立马捡起钥匙，锁好门，爬上楼，回到了自己的卧室，想要平复一下自己的心情，但是她太害怕了，根本无法保持淡定。就在此时，她发现仓库的钥匙沾上了血迹，就想把它擦掉，但试了两三次都没能把血迹擦干净，后来她又用水洗，用肥皂洗，甚至用沙子摩擦，都无济于事。原来，这是一把有魔力的钥匙，一旦沾上血迹永远擦不干净，即使把一面擦干净了，另一面又会重新出现。

当天晚上，蓝胡子回来了，告诉妻子他在回来的路上就收到消息，称他要处理的事情已经圆满解决。妻子想尽一切办法让他相信，对于丈夫这么快回来自己是非常开心的。第二天清晨，蓝胡子向妻子索要钥匙。妻子上前递钥匙时，手一直发抖，所以蓝胡子很容易就猜到发生了什么事。

"仓库的钥匙呢，怎么没和这些钥匙在一起？"他问道。

妻子回复："我肯定是把钥匙落在桌子上了。"

"你还是现在就拿给我吧。"蓝胡子说道。

虽然她再三推脱，但最后还是被迫把钥匙交给了蓝胡子。拿到钥匙的蓝胡子凝神思考了一下，问妻子："钥匙上怎么会有血迹？"

"我不知道，"可怜的妻子说着，面如死灰。

"你不知道？"蓝胡子反问道，"但我非常清楚，你一定进过那间仓库了，对吗？很好，夫人；你是应该进去了，在你看到的那些夫人中间找个位置待着吧。"

听了这话，她立即扑通一声跪在丈夫的脚下，表示自己真心忏悔，祈求他饶恕自己违背了他的禁令。如此漂亮的人儿却神色凄楚，就算是石头也能被她给融化了，然而蓝胡子的心比石头还要硬。

"夫人，你必须得死！"他说道，"现在就得死。"

"既然你一定要杀了我，"妻子泪眼模糊地看着他，说道，"那就给我点时间让我祈祷一下。"

"可以。"蓝胡子回复道，"但只能给你半刻钟的时间，不能再多了。"

妻子一离开蓝胡子，立马把姐姐叫了过来，告诉她："安娜，安娜姐姐(安娜是姐姐的名字)，求求你快去城堡的顶层，看看我的哥哥们来了没有，他们答应我今天会来的。如果你看见他们了，给他们比划手势，让他们快点。"

安娜姐姐来到了城堡的顶层，备受煎熬的妻子不时问安娜，"安娜，安娜姐姐，你看见有人过来了吗？"

安娜姐姐说道："除了光芒万丈的太阳和绿油油的草坪，我什么都没看见。"

与此同时，蓝胡子手里拿着一把锋利的弯刀对妻子大声喊道："赶紧下来，否则，我可要上楼了。"

"求求你了，再给我一会儿时间吧，"妻子回答，随后又对姐姐轻声呼喊，说道："安娜，安娜姐姐，现在呢？你看见有人来了吗？"

安娜姐姐依旧回复："除了光芒万丈的太阳和绿油油的草坪，我什么都没看见。"

"马上给我下来，"蓝胡子喊道，"不然我可上去了。"

"这就来了，"妻子答道，然后又喊："安娜，安娜姐姐，你看见有人过来吗？"

"看见了，"安娜姐姐回复道，"我看见一个大黑团向这边走来了。"

"是我哥哥们吗？"

"唉！不是的，亲爱的妹妹，我看到的原来是一群羊。"

"你是不打算下来了吗？"蓝胡子大喊道。

"再给我一会儿时间，"妻子对蓝胡子说，然后又喊："安娜，安娜姐姐，你看见有人过来吗？"

"我看见了，"姐姐说道，"我看见两个骑兵正在向这边赶过来，但他们离这还有一段路。"

"上帝保佑，"她脱口而出，"是我哥哥们，我正在拼命向他们招手示意，让他们走快点。"

此时蓝胡子怒吼，声音震耳欲聋，仿佛整个城堡都在颤抖。悲惨的妻子只好下楼来，泪流满面、披头散发地跪在蓝胡子的脚下。

"别白费力气了，"蓝胡子说道，"你必须得死。"随后，蓝胡子一手抓住妻子的头发，一手拿着他的弯刀，正准备向她的头部砍去。

可怜的妻子转过身子，用垂死的目光看向蓝胡子，希望蓝胡子能给她一点儿时间，让自己镇静下来。

"不行，不行，"蓝胡子说道，"去上帝那儿报道去吧。"说着就要准备动手。

就在这时，门外响起了猛烈的敲门声，蓝胡子只好立马收手。随后大门被撞开，两个手持长剑的骑士闯了进来，直接向蓝胡子这边飞奔过来。蓝胡子认出这两人就是妻子的哥哥——一个是龙骑兵，一个是火枪手，于是他撒腿就跑，想保住自己的小命。但两兄弟紧跟其后，蓝胡子还没跑到门廊楼梯口就被抓住了，然后兄弟俩举起长剑刺死了蓝胡子。此时，可怜的妻子瘫在地上，吓个半死，根本没有力气站起来迎接哥哥们。

蓝胡子没有继承人，妻子便继承了他的全部财产。而后，妻子把财产的一部分给安娜姐姐筹办婚礼,姐姐嫁给了一个爱慕她很久的年轻绅士;一部分用来帮哥哥们买上尉军官职务;剩下的部分用来筹办自己的婚礼,她后来嫁给了一个真正的绅士,这位绅士帮助她走出了那段嫁给蓝胡子的悲惨岁月。

Blue Beard

Here was a man who had fine houses, both in town and country, a deal of silver and gold plate, embroidered furniture, and coaches gilded all over with gold. But this man had the misfortune to have a blue beard, which made him so frightfully ugly that all the women and girls ran away from him.

One of his neighbors, a lady of quality, had two daughters who were perfect beauties. He desired of her one of them in marriage, leaving to her the choice which of the two she would bestow upon him. They would neither of them have him, and each made the other welcome of him, being not able to bear the thought of marrying a man who had a blue beard. And what besides gave them disgust and aversion, was his having already been married to several wives, and nobody ever knew what became of them.

Blue Beard, to engage their affection, took them, with the lady their mother, and three or four ladies of their acquaintance, with other young people of the neighborhood, to one of his country seats, where they stayed a whole week. There was nothing then to be seen but parties of pleasure, hunting, fishing, dancing, mirth and feasting. Nobody went to bed, but all passed the night in playing tricks upon each other. In short, everything succeeded so well that the youngest daughter began to think the master of the house not to have a beard so very blue, and that he was a mighty civil gentleman. As soon as they returned home, the marriage was concluded.

About a month afterwards Blue Beard told his wife that he was obliged to take a country journey for six weeks at least, about affairs of very great consequence, desiring her to divert herself in his absence, to send for her friends and acquaintances, to carry them into the country, if she pleased, and to make good cheer wherever she was.

"Here," said he, "are the keys of the two great wardrobes, wherein I have my best furniture; these are of my silver and gold plate, which is not every day in use; these open my strong boxes, which hold my money, both gold and silver; these my caskets of jewels; and this is the master key to all my apartments. But for this little one here, it is the key of the closet at the end of the great gallery on the ground floor. Open them all; go into all and every one of them; except that little closet which I forbid you, and forbid it in such a manner that, if you happen to open it, there will be no bounds to my just anger and resentment."

She promised to observe, very exactly, whatever he had ordered. After having embraced her, he got into his coach and proceeded on his journey.

Her neighbors and good friends did not stay to be sent for by the new married lady, so great was their impatience to see all the rich furniture of her house, not daring to come while her husband was there, because of his blue beard which frightened them. They ran through all the rooms, studies and wardrobes, which were all so rich and fine that they seemed to surpass one another.

After that, they went up into the two great rooms, where were the best and richest furniture; they could not sufficiently admire the number and beauty of the tapestry, beds, couches, cabinets, stands, tables, and looking-glasses in which you might see yourself from head to foot; some of them were framed with glass, others with silver, plain and gilded, the finest and most magnificent which were ever seen. They ceased not to extol and envy the happiness of their friend, who in the mean time no way diverted herself in looking upon all these rich things, because of the impatience she had to go and open the closet of the ground floor. She was so much pressed by her curiosity that without considering that it was very uncivil to leave her company, she went down a little back staircase, and with such excessive haste that she had twice or thrice like to have broken her neck.

Being come to the closet door, she made a stop for some time, thinking upon her husband's orders, and considering what unhappiness might attend her if she was disobedient; but the temptation was so strong that she could not overcome it. She took then the little key, and opened it trembling; but could not at first see anything plainly, because the windows were shut. After some moments she began to perceive that the floor was all covered over with clotted blood, in which were reflected the bodies of several dead women ranged against the walls. These were all the wives whom Blue Beard had married and murdered one after another. She was like to have died for fear, and the key, which she pulled out of the lock, fell out of her hand.

After having somewhat recovered her senses, she took up the key, locked the door, and went up stairs into her chamber to recover herself; but she could not, so much was she frightened. Having observed that the key of the closet was stained with blood, she tried twice or three times to wipe it off, but the blood would not come off; in vain did she wash it, and even rub it with soap and sand, the blood still remained, for the key was a fairy, and she could never make it quite clean; when the blood was gone off from one side, it came again on the other.

Blue Beard returned from his journey the same evening, and said, he had received letters upon the road, informing him that the affair he went about was ended to his advantage. His wife did all she could to convince him she was extremely glad of his speedy return. Next morning he asked her for the keys, which she gave him, but with such a trembling hand that he easily guessed what had happened.

"What," said he, "is not the key of my closet among the rest?"

"I must certainly," answered she, "have left it above upon the table."

"Fail not," said Blue Beard, "to bring it to me presently."

After putting him off several times, she was forced to bring him the key. Blue Beard, having very attentively considered it, said to his wife, "How comes this blood upon the key?"

"I do not know," cried the poor woman, paler than death.

"You do not know?" replied Blue Beard. "I very well know, you were resolved to go into the closet, were you not? Mighty well, Madam; you shall go in, and take your place among the ladies you saw there."

Upon this she threw herself at her husband's feet, and begged his pardon with all the signs of a true repentance for her disobedience. She would have melted a rock, so beautiful and sorrowful was she; but Blue Beard had a heart harder than any rock.

"You must die, Madam," said he, "and that presently."

"Since I must die," answered she, looking upon him with her eyes all bathed in tears, "give me some little time to say my prayers."

"I give you," replied Blue Beard, "half a quarter of an hour, but not one moment more."

When she was alone, she called out to her sister, and said to her, "Sister Anne (for that was her name), go up I beg you, to the top of the tower, and look if my brothers are not coming; they promised me that they would come today, and if you see them, give them a sign to make haste."

Her sister Anne went up to the top of the tower, and the poor afflicted wife cried out from time to time, "Anne, sister Anne, do you see anyone coming?"

And sister Anne said, "I see nothing but the sun, which makes a dust, and the grass growing green."

In the mean while Blue Beard, holding a great scimitar in his hand, cried out as loud as he could bawl to his wife, "Come down instantly, or I shall come up to you."

"One moment longer, if you please," said his wife, and then she cried out very softly, "Anne, sister Anne, do you see anybody coming?"

And sister Anne answered, "I see nothing but the sun, which makes a dust, and the grass growing green."

"Come down quickly," cried Blue Beard, "or I will come up to you."

"I am coming," answered his wife; and then she cried, "Anne, sister Anne, do you see anyone coming?"

"I see," replied sister Anne, "a great dust that comes this way."

"Are they my brothers?"

"Alas! No, my dear sister, I see a flock of sheep."

"Will you not come down?" cried Blue Beard.

"One moment longer," said his wife, and then she cried out, "Anne, sister Anne, do you see nobody coming?"

"I see," said she, "two horsemen coming, but they are yet a great way off."

"God be praised," she cried presently, "they are my brothers; I am beckoning to them, as well as I can, for them to make haste."

Then Blue Beard bawled out so loud, that he made the whole house tremble. The distressed wife came down, and threw herself at his feet, all in tears, with her hair about her shoulders.

"Naught will avail," said Blue Beard, "you must die." Then, taking hold of her hair with one hand, and lifting up his scimitar with the other, he was going to take off her head.

The poor lady turning about to him, and looking at him with dying eyes, desired him to afford her one little moment to recollect herself.

"No, no," said he, "recommend yourself to God." And he was just ready to strike.

At this very instant there was such a loud knocking at the gate that Blue Beard made a sudden stop. The gate was opened, and presently entered two horsemen, who were drawing their swords, ran directly to Blue Beard. He knew them to be his wife's brothers, one a dragoon, the other a musketeer; so that he ran away immediately to save himself; but the two brothers pursued so close that they overtook him before he could get to the steps of the porch, when they ran their swords through his body and left him dead. The poor wife was almost as dead as her husband, and had not strength enough to rise and welcome her brothers.

Blue Beard had no heirs, and so his wife became mistress of all his estate. She made use of one part of it to marry her sister Anne to a young gentleman who had loved her a long while; another part to buy captains' commissions for her brothers; and the rest to marry herself to a very worthy gentleman, who made her forget the ill time she had passed with Blue Beard.

林中睡美人

从前有一位国王和王后,为没有子嗣而发愁,愁得难以言表。为了求子,他们四处寻找养生水①,到处祈祷、朝拜,什么办法都试了,但就是不管用。幸运的是,王后最后竟然怀孕了,生下一个女儿。女儿出生后,国王和王后就为女儿举办了一场洗礼盛会,把全国的仙女尽可能都找来(他们共找来了七位)给公主当教母。按照当时仙女的习惯,七位仙女每位都要赠送公主一份礼物。这样,公主就会集所有优点于一身,成为一个完美之人。

洗礼仪式结束后,所有的宾客返回皇宫,那里有为仙女们准备的丰盛晚餐。她们每位面前都放着一个华丽而又精致的全套餐具,一个大金盒里面放着勺子和刀叉。这些餐具也都由黄金打造而成,上面还镶嵌了钻石和红宝石。但当仙女们坐在餐桌前时,她们发现一位没有收到邀请的老仙女正向大厅走来。之所以没有邀请她,是因为老仙女已经搬出仙女塔五十多年了,所有人都以为她要么死了,要么被别人施魔法围住了。随后,国王命令手下给她拿了一套餐具,因为餐具是国王之前专门为七位仙女定制的,所以现在国王无法为她提供和其他七位仙女一样的金盒。为此,老仙女认为自己受到了怠慢,嘴里一直嘟囔着一些威胁性的话语。坐在老仙女旁边的一个小仙女无意中听到了她的抱怨,猜测她很有可能给小公主下诅咒。因而,小仙女等她们起身离席的时候,就躲到帷幔后面,想尽一切办法准备最后一个发言,好最大程度地对老仙女的诅咒进行补救。

---

① 传说中能养生的泉水,不生育是健康欠佳的表现,所以要喝养生水。

与此同时，所有的仙女都开始把各自的礼物赠送给小公主。最小的仙女赠送的是美貌，希望公主成为世界上最漂亮的人；第二个仙女赠送的是智慧，希望公主能拥有天使般的聪明才智；第三个仙女赠送的是优雅，希望公主言行举止优雅动人；第四个仙女赠送的是舞姿，希望公主能够羽衣蹁跹、摇曳生姿；第五个赠送的是声音，希望公主拥有夜莺般的歌喉；第六个赠送的是音乐，希望小公主精通各种乐器。

接下来就轮到老仙女了。她说话的时候直摇头，与其说是因为年纪大，不如说是因为怨气重。她说："公主会被纺锤刺伤手，然后因伤口感染而死。"此话一出，在座的所有人都胆战心惊，不寒而栗，痛哭起来。

就在这时，那位小仙女从帷幔后面走出来，大声说道："请陛下和王后放心，您二位的女儿一定不会这样死去的；虽然我无法完全解除老仙女的诅咒，公主也确实会在使用纺锤纺线时刺伤手，但公主并不会因此而死去，而是因此而长眠一百年。一百年之后，会有一位王子前来将公主唤醒。"

为了避免老仙女的诅咒真的发生，国王立即颁发诏书，规定任何人都不得使用纺纱杆和纺锤纺线，任何人都不得在家私藏纺锤，违令者处死。

大约过去了十五六年，一天国王和王后前往一座城堡中游玩，年轻的小公主就在城堡里跑来跑去，玩得不亦乐乎；她从一个房间跑到另一个房间，最后来到城堡顶楼的一个小房间里，房间里只有一个慈祥的老奶奶正在用纺锤纺线。这位慈祥的老奶奶从未听说过国王对纺锤的禁令。

"奶奶，您在这里做什么呢？"公主问道。

"我正在纺线，我美丽的小人儿，"老奶奶说道，此时她并不知道站在自己面前的就是公主。

"哈!"公主说道,"这真漂亮,您是怎么做的呢?能给我试一下吗?我想看看我能不能和您做得一样好。"不知道是因为纺锤速度加快了,还是公主粗心大意,亦或是老仙女提前安排好的,公主刚把纺锤拿到手上,就刺伤了自己的手,然后昏睡过去。

老太太惊恐万分,不知如何是好,大声呼救。听到求救声,人们从四面八方纷纷赶来,采取各种措施抢救公主:往她脸上泼水,解开她的衣服带子,拍打她的手掌,在她太阳穴位置涂抹匈牙利水(一种内含酒精的香水),但这一切都无法把公主唤醒。

听到嘈杂声,国王也赶了过来,回想起仙女的预言,明白了这件事是无法避免的。于是,国王下令把公主送到皇宫最漂亮的房间,让她躺在一张用黄金白银打造的床上。公主一直昏迷不醒,但依旧如天使般漂亮,容貌丝毫不减:两颊白里透红、容光焕发,嘴唇像涂了胭脂一般红润;虽然眼睛紧闭,但呼吸轻柔。由此可见,公主并没去世,只是昏迷了而已,这令人们欣喜万分。国王下令,任何人不得打扰公主,要让公主好好安睡,直到苏醒。

公主遭遇不幸之时,那位曾拯救公主性命、将死亡换成沉睡一百年的仙女,正待在距离皇宫一万两千里格①的玛塔金王国。此事一出,仙女就从一个穿着七里格靴子的小矮人那里得知了此事。所谓的七里格靴子,就是穿上这种靴子,一步就能走七里格远。仙女得知此事后,即刻出发,乘坐燃烧着熊熊烈火的龙战车于一小时后赶到皇宫。国王亲自迎接,搀扶仙女下车。仙女对国王的安排十分赞同。然而,富有预见的仙女心想,万一公主醒来,发现在这古老的宫殿里只有自己孤零零一个人,一定会感到迷茫、不知所措。于是,仙女就用自己的魔杖将宫殿里的一切(除了国王和王后)都施了法,包括宫廷女教师、女伴、女侍、绅士、大臣、管家、厨师、帮工、助厨、卫士、饲养员、小厮和男仆;她还给马厩里的马匹和

---

① 1 里格约等于 4.8 千米。

马夫、外庭的大狗以及躺在公主床边的漂亮小狗摩西统统都施了魔法。

　　仙女一挥她的魔杖，所有的生命都入睡了，只有在公主醒了之后才会随之醒来，以便随时按需为公主效劳；壁炉里的火苗、炉火上正烤着的鹧鸪和野鸡，甚至连炉火也都沉睡过去。所有的一切都在这一瞬间就完成了，毕竟仙女们做事向来雷厉风行，从不拖沓。

　　国王和王后轻轻地吻别公主，走出了宫殿，即刻下令禁止任何人靠近这所宫殿。其实国王根本没有必要发布命令，因为不到一刻钟的功夫，皇宫花园就被大量新长出来的大大小小的树木、灌木和荆棘包围了，彼此交错形成一道天然的屏障，别说是人，就连野兽都休想跨过去。站在外面的人除了城堡的塔尖，什么都看不见。这确实可以很好地保护公主。毫无疑问，这又出自仙女之手，为的是让公主在沉睡中不受那些好奇者的打扰。

　　一百年过去了，一位来自其他家族并会继承王位的王子来到宫殿附近打猎，看见了屹立于茂密森林之上的城堡塔尖，就打听那是什么地方。随后，人们就把自己听到的传说告诉了王子：有人说那是一个破落的旧城堡，经常闹鬼；有人说那是这个国家的巫师和女巫过安息和夜晚集会的场所；但最普遍的说法就是这里面住着一个食人魔①，他把各地能抓的小孩都抓进这里，这样就可以在空闲时肆无忌惮地吃掉小孩，还不会被人追踪，因为只有他才能穿过这片茂密的森林。

---

① 食人魔是一种体型庞大的巨兽，长着锋利的牙齿，长长的爪子，专吃调皮的小孩。

王子蒙住了，一时不知道到底该相信哪种说法。就在这时，一位村民走过来对他说："尊敬的王子殿下，五十年前我父亲将他从爷爷那听到的这个故事告诉了我。他说，这座城堡里住着一位倾国倾城的公主，不过这位公主必须沉睡一百年，直到一位王子将她唤醒。公主正等着这位王子的到来呢。"听了这些话，年轻的王子蠢蠢欲动，不假思索地认为他能顺利完成这场奇妙的冒险。于是在爱情和荣誉的驱动下，他决定立即前往城堡里面探个究竟。

王子一走向森林，所有参天大树、灌木以及荆棘都纷纷让路，让他顺利通行。原来城堡就坐落于大道的尽头，王子看到后就沿着大道一路向前。然而，令他有点惊讶的是，自己身后竟没有一个随从和士兵跟着，因为他一穿过树林，原本的树木便回归原位，将路挡住了。王子没有因此而退缩，继续勇往直前，年轻而多情的王子总是英勇无比的。接下来，王子来到一个宽敞的外庭，看到眼前的一幕，即使是最英勇无畏的人也会毛骨悚然。空气中弥漫着骇人的静谧，到处都是死亡的景象。放眼望去，看到的只有人和动物的身体静静地躺在那里，仿佛死了一般。但是王子凭借这些守卫红润的脸庞和长了粉刺的鼻子判断，他们只是睡着了而已。而且，他们用的高脚杯中还残留着几滴红酒，清楚地表明他们只是喝醉之后睡着了。

随后，他穿过铺满大理石的院子，走上楼梯，来到了警卫室，卫士们队列整齐且荷枪实弹，但都在呼呼大睡。接着他又经过了几个房间，看到这些房间里到处都是沉睡不醒的绅士和贵妇——有的站着，有的坐着。最后，他来到了一间金

碧辉煌的闺房，看见了此生从未见过的美丽画面：床边帘幔敞开，躺在床上的公主，看上去十五六岁的样子，光彩照人但又自带神圣不可侵犯的光环。王子怀揣仰慕之情，颤颤巍巍地跪在公主身旁。

就在此时，魔法消除，公主完全醒了过来，用无比温柔的目光——比一般人初次见面时的目光更温柔——看向王子说道："是你吗，我的王子？你一定等我很久了吧？"

听到公主这么说，王子顿时心花怒放，而且公主讲话时优雅的神态更是令他神魂颠倒，一时竟忘记了该如何表达自己内心的喜悦和感激之情。王子就向公主保证，今后一定好好地爱她，爱她甚至胜过爱他自己。虽然王子说的话毫无逻辑，语无伦次，也没有华丽的辞藻，但公主还是感到无比开心，因为王子表露了自己对公主最诚挚的爱。显然，王子比公主更加不知所措，毕竟公主有足够多的时间思考她该对王子说些什么。善良的仙女很有可能在公主长睡的日子里，让她做了许多美梦以供她解闷（虽然历史对此只字不提）。最后，他们俩足足聊了四个小时，但他们想说的话才说了不到一半。

与此同时，整个宫殿都复苏了过来，每个人都想起了自己的职责。除了公主和王子，其他人可没有美好的爱情供他们"饱餐一顿"，所以他们都饿得不行。女管家和其他一行人一样，早已饥饿难耐，迫不及待地大声对公主说："请公主就餐！"王子帮忙把公主扶起来，只见公主身着一袭华丽礼服，像极了王子的祖母的穿衣风格——衣服上同样配有一个高领，高领上还有一个点状带的突起，但谨慎的王子并没有把此事告诉公主。尽管衣服款式有点落伍，但公主的美并没有因此而损伤半分。

然后，他们一起走进镶满镜子的大厅，仆人们服侍他们共进晚餐。小提琴手和双簧管手演奏起一百多年前的曲子，这些曲子虽然古老，但依旧悠扬动听。紧接着，晚饭过后，主教便在城堡内的一个小教堂里为他们主持了婚礼，这中间连一分钟都没耽搁。婚礼结束后，王子和公主一回到房间，女管家就为他们拉上了床幔，好让他们休息一会。不过他们根本没怎么睡，公主更不需要睡觉。第二天清晨，王子怕他父皇担心自己的安危，就赶回城去了。王子回到皇宫后，并没有告诉国王实情，只是对他说，自己在森林里狩猎时迷路了，借住在一个矿工的小屋里，矿工拿了一些奶酪和黑面包给自己充饥。

国王为人随和善良，对王子所说的话深信不疑；但他的母后不相信这是真的。看到他几乎每天都出去打猎，而且有时候总有些精心准备的借口，三四晚都不回来，王后就更加确信他一定是在外面有了情人。就这样，王子和公主在一起生活了两年多，有了两个宝宝：一个女儿，一个儿子。因为弟弟比姐姐更俊俏，所以他们给女儿取名晨曦，给儿子取名盛日。

王后为了让王子向她坦露真相，不止一次地对王子说，年轻人就要尽情享乐。但是王子可不敢轻易将自己的秘密告诉她，虽然他爱自己的母后，但也很怕她。因为王后是食人魔的后裔，当初要不是因为她拥有巨额的财富，国王是永远不会娶她的。皇宫有传言说，王后身上继承了食人魔的秉性，一看见小孩子从身边经过，就会情不自禁往他们身上扑，所以王子绝不会向王后透露一个字。

时间一晃又过去了两年，国王因病逝世，王子便继承王位，成了国家的君主。此时，他才向外公布自己的婚姻状况，并为迎接王后举办了盛大典礼，将王后从城堡接回都城。王后坐在两个孩子中间，乘马车回宫，场面十分壮观。

没过多久，国王率兵攻打邻国康塔拉布特王国。这一仗很有可能要持续一整个夏天，于是国王就把国家交给母后管理，并郑重嘱咐她一定要帮他照顾好妻儿。太后为了更加肆无忌惮地满足自己可怕的欲望，待国王一出发就把她的儿媳妇和孩子赶到乡下的一个林中小屋里。

几天后，她也来到了小屋里，对厨师说："明天，我的晚餐就吃小晨曦了。"

"啊？太后！"厨师惊叫道。

"我想吃就吃！"太后用食人魔的口吻说道，表现出对吃鲜肉强烈的欲望，"并且我还要蘸着酱汁①吃。"

可怜的厨师非常清楚，他绝对不可以违背食人魔的意愿，于是拿起他的大刀，向小晨曦的房间走去。此时，四岁的小晨曦一下子跳到厨师的身上，搂住他的脖子，冲他哈哈大笑，向他要糖果吃。看到这一幕，厨师忍不住痛哭起来，大刀也从手中掉了下来，然后他就跑到后院杀了一只小绵羊，并在上面浇上最棒的酱汁好让太后觉得她这辈子都没吃过这么好吃的东西。与此同时，他还将小晨曦送到自己妻子那里，将她藏在院子后面的小屋里。

大约八天后，恶妻的太后又对厨师说："我要吃了小盛日。"

厨师一言不回，因为他已经决定继续用上次的方法骗太后。厨师先去找小盛日，只见年仅三岁的小盛日正手持小花剑戳一只大猴子。厨师将小盛日抱在怀里，将他也送到自己的妻子那里，和姐姐一起藏在小屋里。然后在小盛日的房间里，厨师用一只温顺的小山羊代替小盛日，作为晚餐送给太后。这一次，太后也是对此赞不绝口。

目前为止，一切还比较顺利。只是一天晚上恶妻的太后又对厨师说："我还想吃了王后，还用之前吃孩子用的酱汁。"

---

① 这是一种法式酱汁，主料为洋葱末和煮熟的奶油，然后加入醋、芥末、盐、胡椒和一点红酒。

现在，可怜的厨师对此感到绝望极了，实在想不出可以继续欺骗太后的法子了。王后，就算不加上她沉睡的一百年，也已经二十岁了，虽然皮肤依旧白皙，却已不那么细嫩了。畜圈里哪能找到这样一只肉质相近的动物呢？这真是把他给难住了。然后，他做出决定：杀了王后，保住自己的命。于是在这一想法的驱动下，厨师马上带着匕首来到王后的房间，尽可能假装自己愤怒无比。然而，厨师不愿惊吓她，而是用尊敬的口吻告诉王后，他只是按照太后的命令行事。

"动手吧，动手吧！"她一边将脖子伸向厨师，一边说道，"快执行你的命令吧，这样我就可以去见我的孩子了，我可怜的孩子，我的最爱。"王后以为自己的两个孩子都被吃掉了，因为他们俩都是在她不知情的情况下被带走的。

"不，不要，王后，"可怜的厨师泪流满面地喊道，"您不能死呀，您应该再看看孩子们。他们现在正在我家里待着，是我把他们藏起来了。那么，现在就让我再欺骗太后一次吧，用一只小牝鹿来代替您给太后送去。"

厨师说完就带她来到自己家，王后一见到自己的两个孩子，就上前抱住他们痛哭起来。此时，厨师回到厨房，处理牝鹿，用牝鹿代替王后作为太后的晚餐。太后还以为就是王后，便蘸着酱汁狼吞虎咽地吃起来。太后为自己的残忍行为而沾沾自喜，并且打算到时候国王回来了，就编故事骗他说王后和两个孩子已经被饿狼吃掉了。

一天晚上，太后和往常一样在皇宫的庭院里散步，看看能不能闻到鲜肉的味道。突然间，她听到一间低矮的房间里竟然传来小盛日因淘气而被母亲惩罚的啼哭声，与此同时她还听到了小晨曦为弟弟求情的声音。

食人魔太后此刻听到王后和孩子们的声音，意识到自己被骗了，气得咬牙切齿。第二天清晨她用让人毛骨悚然的语气命令手下，将一口装满了蛤蟆、蝰蛇、水蛇及各种巨蛇的大木桶搬到大院子中央，准备把王后、孩子、女仆、厨师及其妻子扔到大木桶里。此外，太后还下令把王后等人的双手反绑起来，而后再带过来。

于是，王后等人被带了过来，就在刽子手打算把他们都扔到大木桶里的时候，令人意想不到的事情发生了。巡视的国王竟然骑着马回来了，见到这一可怕的场景很震惊，忙问这是要做什么，但谁都不敢回应。食人魔太后见状，气急败坏，暴跳如雷，一头撞进了大木桶，瞬间就被里面的怪物吞食了。

为此，国王也是十分难过的，毕竟她是自己的母亲呀！不过，国王与自己漂亮的妻子及可爱的孩子团聚在一起，很快就得到了安慰。

The Sleeping Beauty in the Wood

There were formerly a king and a queen, who were so sorry that they had no children, so sorry that it cannot be expressed. They went to all the waters in the world; vows, pilgrimages, all ways were tried and all to no purpose. At last, however, the queen proved with child, and was brought to bed of a daughter. There was a very fine christening; and the princess had for her godmothers all the fairies they could find in the whole kingdom (they found seven), that every one of them might give her a gift, as was the custom of fairies in those days, and that by this means the princess might have all the perfections imaginable.

After the ceremonies of the christening were over, all the company returned to the king's palace, where was prepared a great feast for the fairies. There was placed before every one of them a magnificent cover with a case of massive gold, wherein were a spoon, knife and fork, all of pure gold set with diamonds and rubies. But as they were all sitting down at table, they saw come into the hall a very old fairy whom they had not invited, because it was above fifty years since she had been out of a certain tower, and she was believed to be either dead or enchanted. The king ordered her a cover, but could not furnish her with a case of gold as the others, because they had seven only made for the seven fairies. The old fairy fancied she was slighted, and muttered some threat between her teeth. One of the young fairies, who sat by her, overheard how she grumbled; and judging that she might give the little princess some unlucky gift, went, as soon as they rose from the table, and hid herself behind the hangings, that she might speak last, and repair, as much as possible she could, the evil which the old fairy might intend.

In the mean while all the fairies began to give their gifts to the princess. The youngest gave her a gift that she should be the most beautiful person in the world; the next, that she should have the wit of an angel; the third, that she should have a wonderful grace in everything she did; the fourth, that she should dance perfectly well; the fifth, that she should sing like a nightingale; and the sixth, that she should play upon all kinds of music to the utmost perfection.

The old fairy's turn coming next, with a head shaking more with spite than age, she said, that the princess should have her hand pierced with a spindle, and die of the wound. This terrible gift made the whole company tremble, and everybody fell a-crying.

At this very instant the young fairy came out from behind the hangings, and spoke these words aloud, "Be reassured, O king and queen; your daughter shall not die of this disaster: it is true, I have no power to undo entirely what my elder has done. The princess shall indeed pierce her hand with a spindle; but instead of dying, she shall only fall into a profound sleep, which shall last a hundred years; at the expiration of which a king's son shall come and awake her."

The king, to avoid the misfortune foretold by the old fairy, caused immediately proclamations to be made, whereby everybody was forbidden, on pain of death, to spin with a distaff and spindle or to have so much as any spindle in their houses.

About fifteen or sixteen years after, the king and queen being gone to one of their houses of pleasure, the young princess happened one day to divert herself running up and down the palace; when going up from one apartment to another, she came into a little room on the top of a tower, where a good old woman, alone, was spinning with her spindle. This good woman had never heard of the king's proclamation against spindles.

"What are you doing there, Goody?" said the princess.

"I am spinning, my pretty child," said the old woman, who did not know who she was.

"Ha!" said the princess. "This is very pretty; how do you do it? Give it to me, that I may see if I can do so." She had no sooner taken the spindle into her hand, than, whether being very hasty at it, somewhat unhandy, or that the decree of the fairy had so ordained it, it ran into her hand, and she fell down in a swoon.

The good old woman not knowing very well what to do in this affair, cried out for help. People came in from every quarter in great numbers; they threw water upon the princess's face, unlaced her, struck her on the palms of her hands, and rubbed her temples with Hungary-water; but nothing would bring her to herself.

And now the king, who came up at the noise, bethought himself of the prediction of the fairies, and judging very well that this must necessarily come to pass, since the fairies had said it, caused the princess to be carried into the finest apartment in his palace, and to be laid upon a bed all embroidered with gold and silver. One would have taken her for an angel, she was so very beautiful; for her swooning away had not diminished one bit of her complexion; her cheeks were carnation, and her lips like coral; indeed her eyes were shut, but she was heard to breathe softly, which satisfied those about her that she was not dead. The king commanded that they should not disturb her, but let her sleep quietly till her hour of awakening was come.

The good fairy, who had saved her life by condemning her to sleep a hundred years, was in the kingdom of Mata kin, twelve thousand leagues off, when this accident befell the princess; but she was instantly informed of it by a little dwarf, who had boots of seven leagues, that is, boots with which he could tread over seven leagues of ground at one stride. The fairy came away immediately, and she arrived, about an hour after, in a fiery chariot, drawn by dragons. The king handed her out of the chariot, and she approved everything he had done; but, as she had a very great foresight, she thought, when the princess should awake, she might not know what to do with herself, being all alone in this old palace; and this was what she did: She touched with her wand everything in the palace (except the king and the queen), governesses, maids of honor, ladies of the bedchamber, gentlemen, officers, stewards, cooks, under-cooks, scullions, guards, with their beef-eaters, pages, footmen; she likewise touched all the horses which were in the stables, as well as their grooms, the great dogs in the outward court, and pretty little Mosey too, the princess's little spaniel-bitch, which lay by her on the bed.

Immediately upon her touching them, they all fell asleep, that they might not awake before their mistress, and that they might be ready to wait upon her when she wanted them. The very spits at the fire, as full as they could hold of partridges and pheasants, did fall asleep, and the fire likewise. All this was done in a moment. Fairies are not long in doing their business.

And now the king and the queen, having kissed their dear child without waking her, went out of the palace, and put forth a proclamation, that nobody should dare to come near it. This, however, was not necessary; for, in a quarter of an hour's time, there grew up, all round about the park, such a vast number of trees, great and small, bushes and brambles, twining one within another, that neither man nor beast could pass through; so that nothing could be seen but the very top of the towers of the palace; and that too, not unless it was a good way off. Nobody doubted but the fairy gave herein a sample of her art, that the princess, while she continued sleeping, might have nothing to fear from any curious people.

When a hundred years were gone and past, the son of the king then reigning, and who was of another family from that of the sleeping princess, being gone a-hunting on that side of the country, asked, what were those towers which he saw in the middle of a great thick wood? Everyone answered according as they had heard: some said that it was a ruinous old castle, haunted by spirits; others, that all the sorcerers and witches of the country kept there their Sabbath, or nights meeting. The common opinion was that an ogre lived there, and that he carried thither all the little children he could catch, that he might eat them up at his leisure, without anybody's being able to follow him, as having himself, only, the power to pass through the wood.

The prince was at a stand, not knowing what to believe, when a very aged countryman spoke to him, "May it please your Royal Highness, it is now above fifty years since I heard my father, who had heard my grandfather, say that there then was in this castle, a princess, the most beautiful was ever seen; that she must sleep there a hundred years, and should be awaked by a king's son; for whom she was reserved." The young prince was all on fire at these words, believing, without a moment's doubt, that he could put an end to this rare adventure; and pushed on by love and honor resolved that moment to look into it.

Scarce had he advanced towards the wood, when all the great trees, the bushes and brambles, gave way of themselves to let him pass through; he walked up to the castle which he saw at the end of a large avenue which he went into; and what a little surprised him was that he saw none of his people could follow him, because the trees closed again, as soon as he had passed through them. However, he did not cease from continuing his way; a young and amorous prince is always valiant. He came into a spacious outward court, where everything he saw might have frozen up the most fearless person with horror. There reigned over all a most frightful silence; the image of death everywhere showed itself, and there was nothing to be seen but stretched out bodies of men and animals, all seeming to be dead. He, however, very well knew, by the ruby faces and pimpled noses of the beef-eaters, that they were only asleep; and their goblets, wherein still remained some drops of wine, showed plainly, that they fell asleep in their cups.

He then crossed a court paved with marble, went up the stairs, and came into the guard-chamber, where the guards were standing in their ranks, with their muskets upon their shoulders, and snoring as loud as they could. After that he went through several rooms full of gentlemen and ladies, all asleep, some standing, others sitting. At last he came into a chamber all gilded with gold, where he saw, upon a bed, the curtains of which were all open, the finest sight was ever beheld: a princess, who appeared to be about fifteen or sixteen years of age, and whose bright, and in a manner resplendent beauty, had somewhat in it divine. He approached with trembling and admiration, and fell down before her upon his knees.

And now, as the enchantment was at an end, the princess awaked, and looking on him with eyes more tender than the first view might seem to admit of: "Is it you, my prince," said she to him, "you have tarried long."

The prince, charmed with these words, and much more with the manner in which they were spoken, knew not how to show his joy and gratitude; he assured her, that he loved her better than he did himself; his discourse was not well connected, but it pleased her all the more; little eloquence, a great deal of love. He was more at a loss than she, and we need not wonder at it; she had time to think on what to say to him; for it is very probable (though history mentions nothing of it) that the good fairy, during so long a sleep, had entertained her with pleasant dreams. In short, when they talked four hours together, they said not half what they had to say.

In the meanwhile, all the palace awaked; everyone thought upon their particular business; and as all of them were not in love, they were ready to die for hunger; the chief lady of honor, being as sharp set as other folks, grew very impatient, and told the princess aloud that supper was served up. The prince helped the princess to rise, she was entirely dressed, and very magnificently, but his Royal Highness took care not to tell her that she was dressed like his great grandmother, and had a point-band peeping over a high collar; she looked not a bit the less beautiful and charming for all that.

They went into the great hall of looking-glasses, where they supped, and were served by the princess's officers; the violins and haut boys played old tunes, but very excellent, though it was now above a hundred years since they had been played; and after supper, without losing any time, the lord almoner married them in the chapel of the castle, and the chief lady of honor drew the curtains. They had but very little sleep; the princess had no occasion, and the prince left her next morning to return into the city, where his father must have been anxious on his account. The prince told him that he lost his way in the forest, as he was hunting, and that he had lain at the cottage of a collier, who gave him cheese and brown bread.

The king his father, who was of an easy disposition, believed him; but his mother could not be persuaded this was true; and seeing that he went almost every day a-hunting, and that he always had some excuse ready when he had laid out three or four nights together, she no longer doubted he had some little amour, for he lived with the princess above two whole years, and had by her two children, the eldest of which, who was a daughter, was named Aurora, and the youngest, who was a son, they called Day, because he was even handsomer and more beautiful than his sister.

The queen said more than once to her son, in order to bring him to speak freely to her, that a young man must take his pleasure; but he never dared to trust her with his secret; he feared her, though he loved her; for she was of the race of the ogres, and the king would never have married her, had it not been for her vast riches; it was even whispered about the court, that she had ogreish inclinations, and that, whenever she saw little children passing by, she had all the difficulty in the world to refrain from falling upon them. And so the prince would never tell her one word.

But when the king was dead, which happened about two years afterwards; and he saw himself lord and master, he openly declared his marriage; and he went in great ceremony to fetch his queen from the castle. They made a magnificent entry into the capital city, she riding between her two children.

Some time after, the king went to make war with the Emperor Cantalabutte, his neighbor. He left the government of the kingdom to the queen his mother, and earnestly recommended to her care of his wife and children. He was like to be at war all the summer, and as soon as he departed, the queen-mother sent her daughter-in-law and her children to a country-house among the woods, that she might with the more ease gratify her horrible longing.

Some few days afterwards she went thither herself, and said to her clerk of the kitchen, "I have a mind to eat little Aurora for my dinner tomorrow."

"Ah! Madam," cried the clerk of the kitchen.

"I will have it so," replied the queen and this she spoke in the tone of an ogress, who had a strong desire to eat fresh meat, "and will eat her with a Sauce Robert."

The poor man knowing very well that he must not play tricks with the ogress, took his great knife and went up into little Aurora's chamber. She was then four years old, and came up to him jumping and laughing, to take him about the neck, and ask him for some sugar-candy. Upon which he began to weep, the great knife fell out of his hand, and he went into the backyard, and killed a little lamb, and dressed it with such good sauce that his mistress assured him she had never eaten anything so good in her life. He had at the same time taken up little Aurora, and carried her to his wife, to conceal her in the lodging he had at the end of the court yard.

About eight days afterwards, the wicked queen said to the clerk of the kitchen, "I will sup upon little Day."

He answered not a word, being resolved to cheat her, as he had done before. He went to find out little Day, and saw him with a little foil in his hand, with which he was fencing with a great monkey; the child being then only three years of age. He took him up in his arms, and carried him to his wife, that she might conceal him in her chamber along with his sister, and in the room of little Day cooked up a young kid very tender, which the ogress found to be wonderfully good.

This was hitherto all mighty well: but one evening this wicked queen said to her clerk of the kitchen, "I will eat the queen with the same sauce I had with her children."

It was now that the poor clerk of the kitchen despaired of being able to deceive her. The young queen was turned of twenty, not reckoning the hundred years she had been asleep: her skin was somewhat tough, though very fair and white; and how to find in the yard a beast so firm, was what puzzled him. He took then a resolution, that he might save his own life, to cut the queen's throat; and going up into her chamber, with intent to do it at once, he put himself into as great a fury as he could possibly, and came into the young queen's room with his dagger in his hand. He would not, however, surprise her, but told her, with a great deal of respect, the orders he had received from the queen-mother.

"Do it, do it," said she stretching out her neck, "execute your orders, and then I shall go and see my children, my poor children, whom I so much and so tenderly loved." She thought them dead ever since they had been taken away without her knowledge.

"No, no, Madam," cried the poor clerk of the kitchen, all in tears, "you shall not die, and yet you shall see your children again; but it must be in my lodgings, where I have concealed them, and I shall deceive the queen once more, by giving her in your stead a young hind."

Upon this he forthwith conducted her to his chamber; where leaving her to embrace her children, and cry along with them, he went and dressed a hind, which the queen had for her supper, and devoured it with the same appetite, as if it had been the young queen. Exceedingly was she delighted with her cruelty, and she had invented a story to tell the king, at his return, how ravenous wolves had eaten up the queen his wife, and her two children.

One evening, as she was, according to her custom, rambling round about the courts and yards of the palace, to see if she could smell any fresh meat, she heard, in a ground-room little Day crying, for his mamma was going to whip him, because he had been naughty; and she heard, at the same time, little Aurora begging pardon for her brother.

The ogress presently knew the voice of the queen and her children, and being quite mad that she had been thus deceived, she commanded next morning, by break of day (with a most horrible voice, which made everybody tremble) that they should bring into the middle of the great court a large tub, which she caused to be filled with toads, vipers, snakes, and all sorts of serpents, in order to have thrown into it the queen and her children, the clerk of the kitchen, his wife and maid; all whom she had given orders should be brought thither with their hands tied behind them.

They were brought out accordingly, and the executioners were just going to throw them into the tub, when the king (who was not so soon expected) entered the court on horse-back (for he came post) and asked, with the utmost astonishment, what was the meaning of that horrible spectacle? No one dared to tell him; when the ogress, all enraged to see what had happened, threw herself head-foremost into the tub, and was instantly devoured by the ugly creatures she had ordered to be thrown into it for others. The king could not but be very sorry, for she was his mother; but he soon comforted himself with his beautiful wife, and his pretty children.

穿靴子的猫

从前有个磨坊主,只给自己的三个儿子留下了一个磨坊、一头驴和一只猫。很快儿子们就把家产分完了,连公证人和律师都没找,因为他们清楚得很,这些家产连请公证人和律师的酬金都不够。最后老大分到了磨坊,老二分到了驴,老三除了一只猫什么也没分到。

对于自己才分得这么一点可怜的财产,老三心里很不是滋味。

"我的两个哥哥,"他说道,"合伙干的话,就可以过上体面的日子;但是我呢,即使把猫吃了,再用它的皮做个皮手筒暖暖手,最后我还是要被饿死的。"

猫听了这席话,装作若无其事的样子,用沉重而严肃的口吻说道:"我亲爱的主人,你不必烦恼。你只需要给我一个袋子和一双靴子,我就可以跨过泥泞,穿过荆棘。到那时你就会发现,你分到的财产并没有想象中的那么糟糕。"

猫的主人虽然不大相信它的话,但也经常看见它用许多花招抓老鼠:有时倒挂着,有时藏身面粉,装死。因此,对于猫或许能帮助自己改善糟糕的生活状况一事,他仍心存几分希望。

猫得到它要的东西后,勇敢地穿上靴子,把袋子挂在脖子上,用两只前爪抓住袋口的绳子,来到了一个兔子窝旁。它把准备好的米糠和苦苣菜放在袋子里,自己平躺在地上装死,等着一些小兔子自投罗网。一些还不曾见识到社会套路的小兔子,就会傻乎乎地钻进准备好的袋子里面去找吃的。

猫刚刚躺下,就得偿所愿,一只莽撞而又愚蠢的小兔子跳进了它的袋子里。于是它立即拉紧绳子，毫不留情地抓住并勒死了兔子。然后，它就得意洋洋地拎着自己的猎物前往皇宫，要求面见国王。它被带着上了楼梯，来到了国王寝宫，向国王深深鞠了一躬，说道："陛下，这是我的主人卡拉巴斯侯爵（猫咪临时给主人起的爵号）委托我送给陛下的兔子。"国王说道："替我向你的主人传达谢意，就说我对他送的礼物很满意。"

又一天，猫来到了某块未割的玉米地，把袋子敞开放好后自己就躲到了玉米地中间。等两只松鸡跑了进来，它就拉紧绳子，将两只全抓住。和上次送兔子一样，它把松鸡送给了国王。国王兴高采烈地收下了这对松鸡，并赏了它一些喝酒钱。

两三个月以来，猫时不时以主人的名义给国王进献猎物。特别是有一天，它确切得知国王带着女儿——世界上最漂亮的公主——去河边透透气，就对主人说："如果您愿意听我的话，一定会发大财。其实也不需要您做什么，到时候您只要到我指给你的河水位置洗澡就好，剩下的都交给我吧。"

卡拉巴斯侯爵虽然不知道猫葫芦里到底卖的什么药，但还是按照它所说的做了。侯爵正在河里洗着澡，国王恰好经过此地，然后猫就开始拼命地大喊大叫："救命啊，救命啊，我家主人——卡拉巴斯侯爵快要淹死了。"

听到呼喊声，国王从车窗里探出头来，发现呼救的竟然是经常给自己送野味的那只猫，于是吩咐护卫立即把它的主人卡拉巴斯侯爵从河里救上来。

护卫把可怜的侯爵救上来后，猫就走到马车旁，告诉国王刚才它的主人在河里洗澡时，几个小偷来到这儿，尽管它大声喊叫"抓小偷，抓小偷"，小偷还是偷走了主人的衣服。事实上，这只狡猾的猫早就把衣服藏到了一块大石头下面。听了猫的话后，国王立即吩咐随从跑到衣橱里拿一件最合适的衣服递给侯爵。

国王还热情地接见了侯爵。此时，本来就帅气的侯爵，穿着国王赠送的华服，显得极其风度翩翩，公主悄悄地对他产生了好感。而当他恭敬又温柔地看了公主两三眼之后，公主就爱上了他，为他神魂颠倒。随后，国王邀请侯爵同他们一起坐马车去郊游透气。猫看到自己的计划就要成功了，心里乐开了花。不过，谨慎的猫还是一直走在马车的前头打探情况。不一会，它就看见前面有些正在除草的乡下人，便上前对他们说："除草的老百姓们，你们好！如果到时候国王问你们在为谁除草，你们一定要说在为我们的主人卡拉巴斯侯爵除草，否则你们就会被剁成肉沫。"

果然，国王经过此地时就问除草的人，他们是在为谁除草。

"为我们的主人卡拉巴斯侯爵，"遭到猫恐吓的乡下人非常害怕，异口同声地回答。

"真是一块好地，"国王对卡拉巴斯侯爵说。

"是的，陛下，"侯爵说道，"这块草地的收成每年都很好。"

随后，继续向前探路的猫看见一些人正在收玉米，就对他们说："收玉米的老百姓们，你们好！如果到时候国王问你们这是谁的玉米地，你们一定要说是卡拉巴斯侯爵的，否则你们就会被剁成肉沫。"

不一会儿，国王也来到此地，就问他们这块玉米地是谁的。这些人又回答："是我们的主人卡拉巴斯侯爵的。"听到农民的回答，国王又对侯爵夸赞了一番。

一直在前面探路的猫，无论遇见什么人，都对他们说着同样的话。为此，国王对卡拉巴斯侯

爵的大笔财富颇为震惊。

最后猫来到了一座富丽堂皇的城堡前。这座城堡的主人是全世界最富裕的食人魔，国王刚才经过的土地其实都是这个食人魔的财产。猫仔细打听清楚这个食人魔的来历，知道食人魔会干什么之后，就要求面见他，并说既然已经路过此地，如果不能问候一下，就颜面尽失。

食人魔以食人魔族应有的礼数招待它，请它入座。"我想确信一下，"猫说道，"你是否具有百变技能，可以将自己变成你想变成的任何生物。例如，你可以将自己变成一只狮子、大象等类似的生物。"

"是的，"食人魔爽快地答道，"为了让你信服，我现在就可以变成一头狮子给你看。"

猫看见一头狮子就在自己身旁，吓得要命，立马爬到排水槽上，但由于它的靴子并不适合在地板上行走，所以刚才那一举动对它来说又困难又危险。过了一会儿，猫看到食人魔变回原形，这才走下来，承认自己刚才十分害怕。

"此外，我还听说，"猫说道，"你能将自己变成世界上最小的动物，例如大耗子或小家鼠，但我知道要怎么才能相信这是真的。所以，我必须实话跟你说，我认为这是不可能做到的。"

"不可能？"食人魔大声叫道，"那你现在可要看好了。"说着，他就将自己变成了一只老鼠在地板上跑来跑去。猫见状，立即扑上去，吃掉了食人魔。

与此同时，国王经过此处，看到这个富丽堂皇的城堡里，想去参观一下。猫听到外面传来国王的马车走在吊桥上发出的声音后，就跑上去前迎接国王："陛下，欢迎您大驾光临我的主人卡拉巴斯侯爵的城堡。"

"什么？侯爵的？"国王惊讶地说道，"这么说，这座城堡也是你的？中间的主楼及其周围建筑物真是美不胜收，举世无双啊！如果你愿意的话，让我们进去参观一下。"

随后，侯爵挽着公主，跟在国王后面走了进去。他们来到宽敞的大厅，只见早已准备好了丰盛的便餐。这本是食人魔为朋友们当天到访而准备的，只是今天朋友们看见国王在里面，也就没敢进来了。此时，不仅国王的女儿深深地爱上了侯爵，无法自拔，就连国王看到卡拉巴斯侯爵腰缠万贯，而且品质优秀，也十分欣赏他了。国王喝了五六杯酒，对侯爵说道："侯爵，你可愿意做我的驸马？当然这完全得看你自己的意愿。"

为表示感谢，侯爵深深地向国王鞠了几躬，就欣然接受了国王给予的这份殊荣，而且毫不拖延地在同一天就和公主举行了婚礼。就这样，猫也成为了一个大功臣，再也不用去捉老鼠了，只是偶尔消遣娱乐一下罢了。

The Master Cat or Puss in Boots

There was a miller, who left no more estate to the three sons he had, than his mill, his ass, and his cat. The partition was soon made. Neither the scrivener nor the attorney were sent for. They would soon have eaten up all the poor patrimony. The eldest had the mill, the second the ass, and the youngest nothing but the cat.

The poor young fellow was quite comfortless at having so poor a lot.

"My brothers," said he, "may get their living handsomely enough, by joining their stocks together; but for my part, when I have eaten up my cat, and made me a muff of his skin, I must die with hunger."

The cat, who heard all this, but made as if he did not, said to him with a grave and serious air, "Do not thus afflict yourself, my good master; you have only to give me a bag, and get a pair of boots made for me, that I may scamper through the dirt and the brambles, and you shall see that you have not so bad a portion of me as you imagine."

Though the cat's master did not build very much upon what he said, he had however often seen him play a great many cunning tricks to catch rats and mice; as when he used to hang by the heels, or hide himself in the meal, and make as if he were dead; so that he did not altogether despair of his affording him some help in his miserable condition.

When the cat had what he asked for, he booted himself very gallantly; and putting his bag about his neck, he held the strings of it in his two fore paws, and went into a warren where was great abundance of rabbits. He put bran and sow-thistle into his bag, and stretching himself out at length, as if he had been dead, he waited for some young rabbit, not yet acquainted with the deceits of the world, to come and rummage his bag for what he had put into it.

Scarce was he lain down, but he had what he wanted; a rash and foolish young rabbit jumped into his bag, and Monsieur Puss, immediately drawing close the strings, took and killed him without pity. Proud of his prey, he went with it to the palace, and asked to speak with his Majesty. He was showed up stairs into the king's apartment, and, making a low reverence, said to him, "I have brought you, Sir, a rabbit of the warren which my noble lord the Marquis of Carabas (for that was the title which Puss was pleased to give his master) has commanded me to present to your Majesty from him." "Tell your master," said the king, "that I thank him, and that he does me a great deal of pleasure."

Another time he went and hid himself among some standing corn, holding still his bag open; and when a brace of partridges ran into it, he drew the strings, and so caught them both. He went and made a present of these to the king, as he had done before of the rabbit which he took in the warren. The king in like manner received the partridges with great pleasure, and ordered him some money to drink.

The cat continued for two or three months, thus to carry his Majesty, from time to time, game of his master's taking. One day in particular, when he knew for certain that the king was to take the air, along the riverside, with his daughter, the most beautiful princess in the world, he said to his master, "If you will follow my advice, your fortune is made; you have nothing else to do, but go and wash yourself in the river, in that part I shall show you, and leave the rest to me."

The Marquis of Carabas did what the cat advised him to, without knowing why or wherefore. While he was washing, the king passed by, and the cat began to cry out, as loud as he could, "Help, help, my lord Marquis of Carabas is drowning."

At this noise the king put his head out of his coach-window, and finding it was the cat who had so often brought him such good game, he commanded his guards to run immediately to the assistance of his lordship the Marquis of

Carabas.

While they were drawing the poor Marquis out of the river, the cat came up to the coach, and told the king that while his master was washing, there came by some rogues, who went off with his clothes, though he had cried out "Thieves, thieves" several times, as loud as he could. This cunning cat had hidden them under a great stone. The king immediately commanded the officers of his wardrobe to run and fetch one of his best suits for the lord Marquis of Carabas.

The king received him with great kindness, and as the fine clothes he had given him extremely set off his good mien (for he was well made, and very handsome in his person), the King's daughter took a secret inclination to him, and the Marquis of Carabas had no sooner cast two or three respectful and somewhat tender glances, but she fell in love with him to distraction. The king would have him come into his coach, and take part of the airing. The cat, quite overjoyed to see his project begin to succeed, marched on before, and meeting with some countrymen, who were mowing a meadow, he said to them, "Good people, you who are mowing, if you do not tell the king that the meadow you mow belongs to my lord Marquis of Carabas, you shall be chopped as small as mince-meat."

The king did not fail asking of the mowers, to whom the meadow they were mowing belonged.

"To my lord Marquis of Carabas," answered they all together; for the cat's threats had made them terribly afraid.

"Truly a fine estate," said the king to the Marquis of Carabas.

"You see, Sir," said the Marquis, "this is a meadow which never fails to yield a plentiful harvest every year."

The cat, who still went on before, met with some reapers, and said to them, "Good people, you who are reaping, if you do not tell the king that all these corn belongs to the Marquis of Carabas, you shall be chopped as small as mince-meat."

The king, who passed by a moment after, would know to whom all those corn, which he then saw, did belong. "To my lord Marquis of Carabas," replied the reapers; and the king again congratulated the Marquis.

The cat, who went always before, said the same words to all he met; and the king was astonished at the vast estates of my lord Marquis of Carabas.

The cat came at last to a stately castle, the master of which was an ogre, the richest had ever been known; for all the lands which the king had then gone over belonged to this castle. The cat, who had taken care to inform himself who this ogre was, and what he could do, asked to speak with him, saying, he could not pass so near his castle, without having the honor of paying his respects to him.

The ogre received him as civilly as an ogre could do, and made him sit down. "I have been assured," said the cat, "that you have the gift of being able to change yourself into all sorts of creatures you have a mind to; you can, for example, transform yourself into a lion, or elephant, and the like."

"This is true," answered the ogre very briskly, "and to convince you, you shall see me now become a lion."

The cat was so sadly terrified at the sight of a lion so near him that he immediately got into the gutter, not without an abundance of trouble and danger, because of his boots, which were ill-suited for walking upon the tiles. A little while after, when the cat saw that the ogre had resumed his natural form, he came down, and owned he had been very much frightened.

"I have been moreover informed," said the cat, "but I know not how to believe it, that you have also the power to take on you the shape of the smallest animals; for example, to change yourself into a rat or a mouse; but I must own to you, I take this to be impossible."

"Impossible?" cried the ogre. "You shall see that presently." And at the same time he changed into a mouse, and began to run about the floor. The cat no sooner perceived this, but he fell upon him, and ate him up.

Meanwhile the king, who saw, as he passed, this fine castle of the ogre's, had a mind to go into it. The cat, who heard the noise of his Majesty's coach running over the drawbridge, ran out and said to the king, "Your Majesty is welcome to this castle of my lord Marquis of Carabas."

"What! My lord Marquis?" cried the king. "And does this castle also belong to you? There can be nothing finer than this court, and all the stately buildings which surround it; let us go into it, if you please."

The Marquis gave his hand to the princess, and followed the king, who went up first. They passed into a spacious hall, where they found a magnificent collation which the ogre had prepared for his friends, who were that very day to visit him, but dared not to enter knowing the king was there. His Majesty was perfectly charmed with the good qualities of my lord Marquis of Carabas, as was his daughter who was fallen violently in love with him. Seeing the vast estate he possessed, the king said to him, after having drunk five or six glasses: "It will be owing to yourself only, my lord Marquis, if you are not my son-in-law."

The Marquis making several low bows, accepted the honor which his Majesty conferred upon him, and forthwith, that very same day, married the princess. The cat became a great lord, and never ran after mice any more, but only for his diversion.

灰姑娘

从前有一位绅士，再婚娶了第二任妻子，那可是一个极其傲慢的女人，世间罕见。这个女人和前夫生了两个女儿，而且这两个女儿性情和母亲一样，各方面行事都像母亲；而这位绅士和前妻则育有一幼女，不仅心地极其善良，性格温柔，还继承了妈妈的绝世容颜。

婚礼一结束，继母就开始暴露本色。她可受不了继女长得这么漂亮，性格还这么好，她自己的两个女儿可就被比下去了，更显得令人生厌。于是，她就打发继女去干家里最脏最累的活——洗盘子、擦桌子、替她和她的女儿打扫房间。此外，晚上继女还只能睡在一间破旧的阁楼里，将稻草铺平就是床铺。相比之下，继母的两个女儿却睡在精心装饰的房间里，有镶嵌图案的地板、最新款式的床以及一个可以将人从头到脚看个遍的全身镜。

可怜的姑娘也只是默默地忍受着这一切，不敢告诉自己的父亲，害怕父亲到时候会责骂自己，因为现在家里完全是这个妻子掌权。女孩做完家务，常常坐在壁炉边的煤灰上面，时间久了，人们就都叫她"煤球"了。二姐姐因为不似大姐姐那般粗鲁无礼，

就叫她"灰姑娘"。但因为灰姑娘天生丽质，即使衣着朴素，到头来还是比两个身着华丽服饰的姐姐要漂亮百倍。

一天，国王的儿子要举办一场舞会，邀请所有的时尚人士参加。两位小姐也收到了邀请，毕竟她们也是有身份有地位的人。这让她们兴奋不已，赶紧忙着挑选漂亮的外裙、衬裙和头饰，准备到时候艳压群芳。但是，这又给灰姑娘带来了新麻烦，例如，为姐姐们熨平亚麻布料，为礼服缝制荷叶边等，而姐姐们每天除了讨论穿什么，其他一概都不管。"我呢，"大姐姐说道，"到时候就穿法式红色丝绒套装。""我嘛，"二姐姐说道，"我就穿我平时穿的那件衬裙，但要加上一些装饰，外面套上我的那件金花斗篷，并穿钻石胸衣，这样我就可成为世界上最与众不同的人了。"她们还派人去请她们能找到的最出色的梳妆侍女来设计头饰，调整她们自身的双垂片头饰；此外，她们还从精品商买来红画刷和美人斑，以衬托其皮肤白皙。

灰姑娘也被两个姐姐叫去，问她们这身打扮好不好看，因为灰姑娘的审美一向不错。这一次灰姑娘依旧出于好意给她们提了些建议，还主动提出为她们梳头，灰姑娘竟然还会干这个，两姐妹都很乐意灰姑娘帮忙。就在灰姑娘为她们梳头时，突然被问："灰姑娘，你不想去参加舞会吗？"

"啊？"她说道，"别开玩笑了，那可不是我这种人该去的地方。"

"说的没错，"她们说道，"'煤球'参加舞会，一定会让人笑话的。"

要是换作别人听到这种话，一定会把她们的头发弄得乱七八糟的，但灰姑娘没有这么做，她好心地为她们梳了最漂亮的发型。两个姐姐欣喜万分，尽管她们俩已经快两天没有吃东西了，而且还用坏了十多个丝带勒紧自己，以凸显出自己的纤细身材，还要在镜子前照个不停。最后，快乐的日子终于来临了，姐妹俩前去宫廷，灰姑娘目送着她们远去，直到看不见为止。最后灰姑娘终于忍不住，哭了起来。

灰姑娘的教母看见灰姑娘在哭，就问她发生了什么事。

"我想去……我想去……"灰姑娘哭得上气不接下气，话都说不清楚了。

她的这位教母本来就是一个仙女，于是对她说："你非常想去参加舞会，对吗？"

"是……的，"灰姑娘深深地吸了口气，哭着说道。

"好的，"教母说道，"你乖乖的，我就想法子带你去参加舞会。"然后教母就把她带到自己的卧室，对她说："你到菜园里找个南瓜来。"

灰姑娘立马跑到菜园里，摘了一个她能摘到的最好的南瓜送给教母，她无法想象这个南瓜怎么能把她带到舞会上。只见教母把南瓜瓤和肉掏出，只剩下一个外壳。做完这些，教母又用自己的魔杖点了一下南瓜，只见南瓜瞬间变成了一辆金碧辉煌的马车。

接着，教母去看她的捕鼠笼，发现里面有六只生龙活虎的小老鼠。于是，她就让灰姑娘把笼门打开一点，放出小老鼠，同时自己拿起魔杖分别点了点这些小老鼠。顿时，六只小老鼠就变成了六匹带有灰色鼠斑的骏马，站成一排，组成了漂亮的马队。

就差一个车夫了，于是灰姑娘说道："我去看看鼠笼里还有没有大老鼠。如果有的话，倒是可以把它变成车夫。"

"说的对，"教母回答道，"那你快去看看。"

灰姑娘就跑到鼠笼旁，看到里面有三只大老鼠。于是她就把鼠笼递给了教母，教母从中挑选出一只胡子最长的大老鼠，将魔杖一挥，大老鼠就变成了一个和颜悦色的胖车夫，嘴巴上方留着长长的胡须，看上去特别精明。

然后，教母对灰姑娘说："再去菜园里一趟，你会发现水壶后面有六只蜥蜴，把它们给我拿来。"

灰姑娘很快就把六只蜥蜴拿过来，教母把它们变成了六个身着金银相间制服的随从，它们马上蹦跳到马车后面，紧紧跟着，仿佛他们本来就是随从，一辈子就没干过别的事似的。接着，教母对灰姑娘说："好了，一切准备就绪，你可以去参加舞会了，难道不应该开心吗？"

"是的，"灰姑娘哭着说道，"但是我怎么能就这样衣衫褴褛地去参加舞会呢？"

听了她的话，教母用自己的魔杖点了一下她，转眼间，灰姑娘破旧的衣服就变成了镶满珠宝的金银礼服，旧鞋也变成世界上最漂亮的水晶鞋。

这样打扮好之后，灰姑娘坐上马车准备出发。此时教母告诉她必须在夜里十二点之前回来，否则一旦过了十二点，这所有的一切都会变回原形，马车就会变回南瓜模样，骏马就会变回小老鼠，车夫就会变回大老鼠，随从就会变回蜥蜴，衣服也会变成最初破烂不堪的样子。

灰姑娘向教母承诺一定会在十二点之前回来，然后就驾着马车参加舞会去了，兴奋之情溢于言表。有人告诉王子，来了一位陌生的美丽公主，谁都不认识。听闻此言，王子就跑过来亲自迎接她，扶她下马车，在众人的陪同下将她迎入大厅。瞬间，整个大厅鸦雀无声，所有人都目不转睛地注视着这个陌生女孩的盛世容颜，就连跳舞的人们也停下了自己的舞步，小提琴演奏者也停下了手中的琴弦。此时大厅里唯一的能听到的声音，就是不断的赞美声："啊，她真的太漂亮了！啊，她真的太漂亮了！"

国王年事已高，但还是忍不住暗送秋波，并轻轻地对王后说自己已经好久没有见过这样倾国倾城的可人儿了。所有的夫人小姐们都忙着打量她的衣服和头饰，并在心里打定主意，要是能买到这么漂亮的布料和头饰，找到这么出色的裁缝和发型师，明天也要如此装扮。

王子先是将她领到最尊贵的位子上，随后又邀请她跳舞。人们见她翩翩起舞，舞姿如此优雅动人，对她更是赞不绝口。随后，国王为大家准备了点心，但是年轻的王子哪里还顾得上吃东西，只是目不转睛地盯着她看。灰姑娘走过去和姐姐们坐到一起，温文尔雅地把王子送给她的橙子和构橼西瓜分给姐姐们。这让两个姐姐大吃一惊，因为她们根本就没有认出灰姑娘来。

正当灰姑娘和姐姐们玩得不亦乐乎的时候，突然听到了十一点四十五分的钟声，然后她立即起身跟众人告别，就拼命地往外跑去。

她一回到家，就跑去找自己的教母，向她表示感谢。此外她还跟教母说，自己由衷地希望明天还能去参加舞会，因为王子已经对她一见倾心了。当她热切地告诉教母舞会上所发生的事时，她的两个姐姐敲门，灰姑娘跑过来打开门。

"你们怎么玩那么久，才回来啊？"灰姑娘一边大声说，一边目瞪口呆地看着，揉了揉眼睛，并伸了伸胳膊，就像刚刚睡醒一样。但其实，自从她们走后，她一刻都没有睡过。

"你要是参加舞会了，"一个姐姐说道，"肯定也会乐此不疲的。舞会上来了一位漂亮的公主，绝对是举世无双。在舞会上，她不仅对我们彬彬有礼，还送了我们橙子和构橼西瓜呢。"听了姐姐们的夸赞，灰姑娘非常开心，就问她们公主叫什么。两个姐姐说，她们不知道这位公主的名字，为此王子也是颇感烦恼，想要向全世界打听这位公主。这时，灰姑娘笑着回复道："那么，她一定真的超级漂亮。天哪，你们真是太幸运了，我要是也能和她见一面该多好！哈！亲爱的夏洛特小姐，你能把你平时每天穿的那件黄色礼服借我穿一下吗？"

"咦，想得美！"夏洛特小姐尖叫道，"把我的衣服借给你这么一个煤球？谁会傻到这种地步？"

灰姑娘其实早就想到会有这样的回答，所以听到她的拒绝反而松了一口气；如果姐姐因为一句玩笑话，就把衣服借给她的话，那她就真的不知如何是好了。

第二天，两个姐姐同样来到了舞会现场，灰姑娘也来了，并且穿得比昨天更华丽。王子时刻陪伴在灰姑娘左右，不停地赞美她，向她说着甜言蜜语，灰姑娘因此沉醉其中而无法自拔，以致于完全忘记了教母对自己的警示，还以为最多到了十一点钟，直到午夜十二点钟声敲响的那一刻，她才意识到原来已经十二点了。于是，灰姑娘便如小鹿一般敏捷，起身拔腿就跑。

王子见状追了上去，只是没能追上她。中途，灰姑娘跑丢了一只水晶鞋，被王子小心翼翼地拾起，带了回去。灰姑娘回到家时已经累得气喘吁吁，没有了马车和随从，衣服也变得破旧不堪，刚才的那般雍容华贵也早已消失殆尽，只剩下一只鞋子。此时，王子已派人去询问守卫城门的士兵，问刚才有没有看见一位公主从这跑了出去。士兵回复，他们只看见一个衣着破旧的小姑娘跑了出去，看样子不是什么小姐，顶多就是一个贫穷的村姑。

两个姐姐从舞会回来之后，灰姑娘就去问她们是否玩得很开心，漂亮公主是否也去参加了舞会。他们告诉灰姑娘，漂亮公主的确去参加舞会了，但是十二点的钟声一响，她就匆匆忙忙地跑掉了，并且由于她跑得太着急了，竟然掉了一只水晶鞋——世界上最漂亮的鞋子。王子捡到这只水晶鞋之后，在舞会后半程就什么都不做，只是直直地盯着水晶鞋发呆。可见，他一定是爱上了水晶鞋的主人了。

事情确实如她们所说的那样。没过几天，王子就昭告天下：谁能穿上这只水晶鞋，他就要谁为妻。最初，王子派人请公主们过来试一试，然后又让公爵家的小姐们一个接一个地试穿，最后整个宫廷的小姐都试了个遍，但都没有找到能穿上这只水晶鞋的人。最后，王子派人将鞋子送给灰姑娘的两个姐姐，两个姐姐纵然使出浑身解数，最终也只是白费力气。

灰姑娘看到后，一眼就认出了那只水晶鞋，笑着对她们说："让我试一下吧？看看我穿起来是不是正合适？"

听了灰姑娘的话，两个姐姐哈哈大笑起来，并开始嘲讽她。不过此时，送鞋子的这位谦谦君子，认真审视了一下灰姑娘，发现这位姑娘长得如此精致，就说既然自己奉命让每个人都试穿一下这只水晶鞋，那么她也应该试穿。然后，他就邀请灰姑娘坐下，并把水晶鞋送到了灰姑娘脚边，只见灰姑娘毫不费力，一下子就穿上了水晶鞋，大小刚刚好，仿佛鞋子就像蜡做的一般。两个姐姐看得目瞪口呆，但更让两个姐姐吃惊的是，灰姑娘竟然从她的袋子里拿出了鞋子的另一只，穿在了脚上。随即，教母走了进来，用她的魔杖轻轻碰了一下灰姑娘的衣服，只见她现在身上穿的这件礼服比之前更加雍容华贵。

两个姐姐这才认出灰姑娘就是当时舞会上见到的那位漂亮公主，她们立即跪在她的脚下，并祈求灰姑娘能原谅自己之前对她的恶劣行为。灰姑娘将她们俩扶起来，和她们抱在一起，哭着说自己已经真心原谅她们了，并希望以后她们能永远爱自己。

装扮完毕后，灰姑娘就被接到了王子面前。再次见到灰姑娘，王子觉得她越发迷人了。几天后，灰姑娘和王子就举行了婚礼。

灰姑娘不仅漂亮，而且心地善良。婚后，灰姑娘便把两个姐姐接入了皇宫，并在当天为她们和两位宫廷贵族举办了婚礼。

Cinderilla or the Little Glass Slipper

Once there was a gentleman who married, for his second wife, the proudest and most haughty woman that was ever seen. She had, by a former husband, two daughters of her own humor and they were indeed exactly like her in all things. He had likewise, by another wife, a young daughter, but of unparalleled goodness and sweetness of temper, which she took from her mother, who was the best creature in the world.

No sooner were the ceremonies of the wedding over, but the stepmother began to show herself in her colors. She could not bear the good qualities of this pretty girl; and the less, because they made her own daughters appear the more odious. She employed her in the meanest work of the house; she scoured the dishes, tables, and rubbed Madam's chamber, and those of Misses, her daughters; she lay up in a sorry garret, upon a wretched straw-bed, while her sisters lay in fine rooms, with floors all inlaid, upon beds of the very newest fashion, and where they had looking-glasses so large that they might see themselves at their full length, from head to foot.

The poor girl bore all patiently, and dared not tell her father who would have rattled her off, for his wife governed him entirely. When she had done her work, she used to go into the chimney-corner, and sit down among cinders and ashes, which made her commonly be called Cinder-breech; but the youngest, who was not so rude and uncivil as the eldest, called her Cinderilla. However, Cinderilla, notwithstanding her mean apparel, was a hundred times handsomer than her sisters, though they were always dressed very richly.

It happened that the king's son gave a ball, and invited all persons of fashion to it. Our young misses were also invited, for they cut a very grand figure among the quality. They were mightily delighted at this invitation, and wonderfully busy in choosing out such gowns, petticoats, and head-clothes as might best become them. This was a new trouble to Cinderilla, for it was she who ironed her sisters' linen, and plaited their ruffles; they talked all day long of nothing but how they should be dressed. "For my part," said the eldest, "I will wear my red velvet suit, with French trimming." "And I," said the youngest, "shall only have my usual petticoat; but then, to make amends for that, I will put on my gold-flowered manteau, and my diamond stomacher, which is far from being the most ordinary one in the world." They sent for the best tire-woman they could get, to make up their head-dresses, and adjust their double-pinners, and they had their red brushes, and patches from the fashionable maker.

Cinderilla was likewise called up to them to be consulted in all these matters, for she had excellent notions, and advised them always for the best, nay and offered her service to dress their heads, which they were very willing she should do. As she was doing this, they said to her, "Cinderilla, would you not be glad to go to the ball?"

"Ah!" said she. "You only jeer at me; it is not for such as I am to go thither."

"You are in the right of it," replied they, "it would make the people laugh to see a Cinder-breech at a ball."

Anyone but Cinderilla would have dressed their heads awry, but she was very good, and dressed them perfectly well. They were almost two days without eating, so much they were transported with joy; they broke above a dozen of laces in trying to be laced up close that they might have a fine slender shape, and they were continually at their looking-glass. At last the happy day came; they went to court, and Cinderilla followed them with her eyes as long as she could, and when she had lost sight of them she fell a-crying.

Her godmother, who saw her all in tears, asked her what was the matter.

"I wish I could—, I wish I could—;" she was not able to speak the rest, being interrupted by her tears and sobbing.

This godmother of hers, who was a fairy, said to her, "You wish you could go to the ball, is it not so?"

"Y—es," cried Cinderilla, with a great sigh.

"Well," said her godmother, "be but a good girl, and I will contrive that you shall go." Then she took her into her chamber, and said to her, "Run into the garden, and bring me a pumpkin."

Cinderilla went immediately to gather the finest she could get, and brought it to her godmother, not being able to imagine how this pumpkin could make her go to the ball. Her godmother scooped out all the inside of it, leaving nothing but the rind; which done, she struck it with her wand, and the pumpkin was instantly turned into a fine coach, gilded all over with gold.

She then went to look into her mouse-trap, where she found six mice all alive, and ordered Cinderilla to lift up a little the trap-door, when giving each mouse, as it went out, a little tap with her wand, the mouse was at that moment turned into a fair horse, which altogether made a very fine set of six horses of a beautiful mouse-colored dapple-grey.

Being at a loss for a coachman, "I will go and see," says Cinderilla, "if there be never a rat in the rat-trap, that we may make a coachman of him."

"You are in the right," replied her godmother; "go and look."

Cinderilla brought the trap to her, and in it there were three huge rats. The fairy chose one of the three, which had the largest beard, and, having touched him with her wand, he was turned into a fat jolly coachman who had the smartest whiskers eyes ever beheld.

After that, she said to her, "Go again into the garden, and you will find six lizards behind the watering pot; bring them to me."

She had no sooner done so, but her godmother turned them into six footmen, who skipped up immediately behind the coach, with their liveries all bedaubed with gold and silver, and clung as close behind it, as if they had done nothing else their whole lives. The fairy then said to Cinderilla, "Well, you see here an equipage fit to go to the ball with; are you not pleased with it?"

"O yes," cried she, "but must I go thither as I am, in these poison nasty rags?"

Her godmother only just touched her with her wand, and, at the same instant, her clothes were turned into cloth of gold and silver, all beset with jewels. This done she gave her a pair of glass-slippers, the prettiest in the whole world.

Being thus decked out, she got up into her coach; but her godmother, above all things, commanded her not to stay till after midnight, telling her at the same time that if she stayed at the ball one moment longer, her coach would be a pumpkin again, her horses mice, her coachman a rat, her footmen lizards, and her clothes become just as they were before.

She promised her godmother, she would not fail of leaving the ball before midnight; and then away she drove, scarce able to contain herself for joy. The king's son who was told that a great princess whom nobody knew came ran out to receive her; he gave her his hand as she alighted out of the coach, and led her into the hall, among all the company. There was immediately a profound silence, they left off dancing, and the violins ceased to play, so attentive was everyone to contemplate the singular beauty of this unknown new comer. Nothing was then heard but a confused noise of, "Ha! How handsome she is! Ha! How handsome she is!"

The king himself, old as he was, could not help ogling her, telling the queen softly that it was a long time since he had seen so beautiful and lovely a creature. All the ladies were busied in considering her clothes and head-dress that they might have some made next day after the same pattern, provided they could meet with such fine materials, and as able hands to make them.

The king's son conducted her to the most honorable seat, and afterwards took her out to dance with him: she danced so very gracefully that they all more and more admired her. A fine collation was served up, whereof the young prince ate not a morsel, so intently was he busied in gazing on her. She went and sat down by her sisters, showing them a thousand civilities, giving them part of the oranges and citrons which the prince had presented her with; which very much surprised them, for they did not know her.

While Cinderilla was thus amusing her sisters, she heard the clock strike eleven and three-quarters, whereupon she immediately made a curtsey to the company, and hasted away as fast as she could.

Being got home, she ran to seek out her godmother, and after having thanked her, she said she could not but heartily wish she might go next day to the ball, because the king's son had desired her. As she was eagerly telling her godmother whatever had passed at the ball, her two sisters knocked at the door which Cinderilla ran and opened.

"How long you have stayed," cried she, gaping, rubbing her eyes, and stretching herself as if she had been just awaked out of her sleep; she had not, however, any manner of inclination to sleep since they went from home.

"If you had been at the ball," said one of her sisters, "you would not have been tired with it; there came thither the finest princess, the most beautiful ever was seen with mortal eyes; she showed us a thousand civilities, and gave us oranges and citrons." Cinderilla was transported with joy; she asked them the name of that princess; but they told her they did not know it; and that the king's son was very anxious to learn it, and would give all the world to know who she was. At this Cinderilla, smiling, replied, "She must then be very beautiful indeed; Lord! How happy have you been! Could not I see her? Ah! Dear Miss Charlotte, do lend me your yellow suit of clothes which you wear every day!"

"Ay, to be sure!" cried Miss Charlotte. "Lend my clothes to such a dirty Cinder-breech as you are; who's the fool then?"

Cinderilla, indeed, expected some such answer, and was very glad of the refusal, for she would have been sadly put to it, if her sister had lent her what she asked for jestingly.

The next day the two sisters were at the ball, and so was Cinderilla, but dressed more magnificently than before. The king's son was always by her, and never ceased his compliments and amorous speeches to her; to whom all this was so far from being tiresome that she quite forgot what her godmother had recommended to her so that she, at last, counted the clock striking twelve, when she took it to be no more than eleven; she then rose up, and fled as nimble as a deer.

The prince followed, but could not overtake her. She left behind one of her glass slippers, which the prince took up most carefully. She got home, but quite out of breath, without coach or footmen, and in her nasty old clothes, having nothing left her of all her finery, but one of the little slippers, fellow to that she dropped. The guards at the palace gate were asked if they had not seen a princess go out. They said they had seen nobody go out, but a young girl, very meanly dressed, and who had more the air of a poor country wench, than a gentle-woman.

When the two sisters returned from the ball, Cinderilla asked them if they had been well diverted, and if the fine lady had been there. They told her yes, but that she hurried away immediately when it struck twelve, and with so much haste that she dropped one of her little glass slippers, the prettiest in the world, and which the king's son had taken up; that he had done nothing but look at it during all the latter part of the ball, and that most certainly he was very much in love with the beautiful person who owned the little slipper.

What they said was very true; for a few days after, the king's son caused it to be proclaimed by sound of trumpet that he would marry her whose foot this slipper would just fit. They whom he employed began to try it on upon the princesses, then the duchesses, and all the court, but in vain. It was brought to the two sisters, who did all they possibly could to thrust their feet into the slipper, but they could not effect it.

Cinderilla, who saw all this, and knew her slipper, said to them laughing, "Let me see if it will not fit me?"

Her sisters burst out a-laughing, and began to banter her. The gentleman who was sent to try the slipper, looked earnestly at Cinderilla, and finding her very handsome, said it was but just that she should try, and that he had orders to let everyone make try all. He invited Cinderilla to sit down, and put the slipper to her foot, he found it went on very easily, and fitted her, as if it had been made of wax. The astonishment her two sisters were in was excessively great, but still abundantly greater, when Cinderilla pulled out of her pocket the other slipper, and put it on her foot. Thereupon, in came her godmother, who having touched, with her wand, Cinderilla's clothes, made them richer and more magnificent than any of those she had before.

And now her two sisters found her to be that fine beautiful lady whom they had seen at the ball. They threw themselves at her feet, to beg pardon for all the ill treatment they had made her undergo. Cinderilla took them up, and as she embraced them, cried that she forgave them with all her heart, and desired them always to love her.

She was conducted to the young prince, dressed as she was; he thought her more charming than ever, and, a few days after, married her.

Cinderilla, who was no less good than beautiful, gave her two sisters lodgings in the palace, and that very same day matched them with two great lords of the court.

小凤头里凯

从前,有一位王后生了一个奇丑无比的儿子,为此人们一直议论纷纷:这个孩子到底还有没有点人样。然而,一位仙女在孩子一出生时就声称,这个孩子长大后一定会非常招人喜欢,因为他拥有超乎寻常的聪明才智。此外,仙女还补充道,她刚刚赋予男孩一种能力,男孩可以把自己的聪明才智分享给他最爱的人,而且只要他乐意,他想分享多少就分享多少。生了这么一个奇丑无比的孩子,可怜的王后也是十分苦恼,不过现在仙女的话多多少少给她带来了一丝安慰。事情确实如仙女所说的那样,男孩刚会闲扯,就讲述各种奇妙的事情,一举一动都展示着聪明才智,散发出迷人的魅力。差点忘了告诉你们,男孩刚出生时,头上长着一簇头发,看上去像个凤冠一般,加上他姓里凯,所以大家都叫他小凤头里凯。

七八年后,邻国王后生下一对双胞胎女儿。大女儿刚生下来就是一个无可比拟的美人胚子,为此王后高兴得忘乎所以,难免让在场的人担心她会乐极生悲。当初,曾在小凤头里凯出生时赠予他能力的那位仙女也在现场,为防止王后因公主的美貌而高兴过头,就说大公主一点智慧都没有,相反她长得越漂亮就会变得越愚蠢。此话一出,王后立马被泼了一盆冷水,窘迫极了,但更令她伤心的是,随即出生的二女儿竟奇丑无比。

"王后,你没必要因此而伤心难过,"仙女说道,"您的二女儿将异常聪慧,以至于人们会忽略她的外貌。"

"上帝保佑,"王后回复道,"但是有没有什么办法能让漂亮的大女儿变得聪明一点呢？"

"对于赋予大公主智慧这件事，王后，我实在是无能为力，"仙女回答，"除了给予她美貌，我实在是没有办法满足您的其他愿望。不过，我可以赋予她一种本领，有了这一本领她就可以让自己的心仪男子变得英俊潇洒。"

随着两位公主慢慢地长大，她们各自的优点愈发突出，大家纷纷称赞大公主倾国倾城，小公主聪明伶俐。但与此同时，她们的缺点也随着年龄增长而愈发明显，小公主肉眼可见越长越丑，大公主则越长越蠢。对于别人问的问题，大公主要么直接一言不发，要么净说一些傻话。平时做事更是笨手笨脚的，即使是将四个陶器放到壁炉上这么简单的事，她都做不好，非得打碎一个不可；就连喝水都能泼洒一半，把衣服弄湿。尽管对年轻人而言，天生丽质具有很大优势，但是在宾客面前，丑陋的妹妹却总能占姐姐的上风。一开始人们确实更关注姐姐的美貌，忍不住跑去赞赏她，但不一会儿人们就会纷纷聚到妹妹的周围，听她讲各种令人愉快的娱乐趣事。不到一刻钟的功夫，人们就会惊奇地发现，姐姐那边已经空无一人，反观妹妹这边早已座无虚席。虽然姐姐莫名的愚钝，但还是发现了其中的缘由，她宁愿用自己全部的美貌换取妹妹一半的智慧。虽然王后平时比较谨慎，但有几次还是忍不住责备姐姐。这让可怜的姐姐十分郁闷，甚至差点因为悲伤过度而死。

一天，大公主在林中哀叹自己的不幸，突然看见迎面走来一个衣着华丽、令人讨厌的小男孩，正是小凤头里凯。原来公主的画像随处可见，小凤头里凯看到大公主的画像后就爱上了她，于是就离开父王的国度去寻找她，希冀遇见她，并且还能同她讲话。

看到大公主独自一人，里凯内心甚是欣喜若狂，就彬彬有礼地走到她身边，向她表白自己的仰慕之情，却发现她如此郁郁寡欢，就问道："小姐，我不理解，像你这么漂亮的人，还有什么事儿能让你这么伤心呢？毫不夸张地说，我见过无数漂亮迷人的小姐和夫人，但从未见过一个比得上你呢。"

"你说笑了，"大公主回了一句后，就不再说话了。

"在我看来，美貌，"小凤头里凯回复道，"可是一大优势，它可以取代任何东西。你既然都拥有了美貌，我看没什么事能让人很烦心。"

"唉，"大公主哭着说道，"我宁愿像你一样外貌丑陋，但拥有智慧，也不愿像我现在一样，美丽却愚蠢。"

"小姐，没有什么比认为自己缺少智慧更能说明自己富有智慧的了，"小凤头里凯回复说道，"越是聪明的人越是觉得自己缺少智慧。这是优秀的品质。"

"我不懂这个道理，"大公主说道，"但是我非常清楚，自己太笨了。这让我很是苦恼，要是继续下去，差不多能要我的小命。"

"如果那就是令你苦恼的全部，我完全可以帮你消除。"

"那么你怎么帮我呢？"大公主哭着问。

"我拥有一种本领，"小凤头里凯回答道，"可以把我自己的智慧分享给我最爱的人。小姐，而你就是这个人。如果你愿意嫁给我，你就可以像我一样聪明，当然这还得看你的意愿。"

里凯的话让大公主颇为震惊，一时说不出话来。

"看来，"小凤头里凯继续说道，"这个提议让你感到为难了，很正常。我会给你一年的时间来考虑这件事的。"

大公主十分渴望能拥有一些智慧，但是与此同时，她又十分愚蠢，认为一年的时间永远都不会过完，所以就答应了小凤头里凯的提议——一年之后的今天嫁给他。她刚一答应里凯，就发现自己像变了一个人似的。现在的她可以随心所欲，想说什么就说什么，而且说起话来温文尔雅，轻松又自然。这时起，她直接和小凤头里凯对话，滔滔不绝，口若悬河，就连小凤头里凯都觉得自己赋予公主的智慧甚至超过了自己。

　　大公主回宫后，人们都为她突如其来的巨大转变所震惊：现在她讲话不仅充满了智慧，而且非常幽默风趣，与之前的愚蠢无礼截然不同。宫廷里所有人都对这件超乎想象的事情感到高兴，唯独妹妹心里不自在，因为这样一来自己的智慧就不再占有优势了，从此在姐姐身边自己就真的只是一个丑小妞了，不会再受人待见。现在，国王无论做什么事都听取姐姐的意见，有时候甚至还会在姐姐的房间召开议会。大公主突然变聪明的事儿传开后，邻国所有的年轻王子都努力讨取她的欢心，几乎每一个人都向她求婚。但是大公主发现他们都没有自己聪明，于是给他们一个解释机会，但还是把他们都给拒绝了。

　　然而有一天，宫里来了一位位高权重、富甲一方、足智多谋、英俊潇洒的男子，不免让大公主心动。国王看穿了大公主的小心思，便对她说，选择夫君、宣布结婚这些事儿完全由她自己做主。然而，一个人越有头脑，考虑得就会越多，也就越难在感情这种事情上下定决心，于是大公主向父王表示感谢后，希望父王再多给她一些时间，好好考虑一下这件事儿。

　　一天，大公主为了方便思考到底该如何解决这件事儿，就出来漫步，最后竟然不知不觉地来到了同小凤头里凯见面的小树林。就当她边沉思边走时，她突然听到脚下传来嘈杂的声音，仿佛好多人在来回走动，急着做什么事一样。于是，她竖起耳朵，认真倾听，就听到有人说"把锅递给我！"，又有人说"把壶递给我"，第三个人又说"火上再加些柴禾"。

此时，地面突然裂出一个通道，公主似乎看见了她的脚下出现一个超大的厨房，里面有主厨、帮厨以及其他各类人员，正在着手准备丰盛的招待宴席。随后，约二三十个烘烤人员又从厨房里走出来，手里拿着肥肉馅灌注针，帽子上放着串肉杆，走进一条漂亮的林间小巷，围在一张长长的桌子旁边，一边哼着悦耳的歌曲，一边有节奏地干着活儿。

公主见到这番情景，觉得很惊讶，就上前去打听他们是为谁服务。

"当然是为了里凯王子啰，"厨师长说道，"王子明天就要结婚啦。"

听了厨师长的话，大公主感到更加诧异。就在这时，她回想起正是一年前的今天，自己许诺一年后要嫁给里凯王子。想到这里，大公主不免惊慌失措起来，好像要跌倒在地。

她之所以忘了这件事，是因为她当初许下承诺的时候自己还很傻，在获得王子赋予的很多智慧后自然也就把自己说过的傻话忘得一干二净了。接下来，她继续向前走，还没走到三十步就见小凤头里凯迎面而来，英勇无畏，衣着华丽，就像一个即将迎娶新娘的王子。

"你看，公主，"他说道，"我是非常信守承诺的，至少没有一丝犹豫。我相信你来这儿，也是履行诺言嫁给我，让我成为世界上最幸福的人，对吗？"

"坦率地说，"大公主回复道，"我还没有对此事做出任何决定，而且我也绝对不信，自己会做出你所希望的那种决定。"

"你真是让我大吃一惊，公主。"小凤头里凯说道。

"我相信，"大公主说道，"并且坚信，如果我是同一位小丑或是一位傻子讲话，那么我现在肯定会不知所措，因为他会说'公主说话，是一定算数的；你已经答应了我，就一定要嫁我不可'。但我现在是同世界上最理智、最具判断力的人交谈，那么我确信他一定会听我把道理讲完。你也知道，当初我只是一个傻孩子，尽管如此，我都无法做出决定是否要嫁给你；现在我拥有了你所赋予我的判断力，比以前更难以取悦了，你又怎能指望我做出当初都无法做出的决定呢？要是你真心想让我嫁给你，那么当初你赋予我智慧，让我看事情更透彻，真是大错特错了。"

"如你所说，"小凤头里凯反驳道，"如果一个又不聪明又不理智的人指责你失信于人，你都能接受的话，那么在这样一件关乎我自己人生幸福的大事上，为什么你却要求我放弃对你的责问呢？是不是智者应该比傻子低一等才算合理呢？这就是你说的道理吗？过去你那么渴望得到智慧，难道拥有很多智慧后就要这样看问题吗？好吧，还是让我们说点实际的吧。除了外表丑陋和身体畸形，我还有什么地方让你生厌吗？对我的出身、智慧、幽默或举止，你难道不满意吗？"

"不，"大公主回答道，"你刚才说的这些，让我喜欢你，尊敬你。""如果这样的话，"小凤头里凯说道，"我就高兴了，因为你完全有能力把我变成世界上最英俊的人。"

"我怎么才能做得到呢？"大公主问道。

"只要你足够地喜欢我，"小凤头里凯说道，"喜欢到希望我变得英俊，然后就能变成现实了。为了让你相信我说的话，我可以告诉你：就在我出生的那一天，一位仙女赋予我一种本领——能把我所喜欢的人变得极其聪明；同样是这位仙女，用了同样的方法赋予了你另外一种本领——能让你喜欢的人变极其英俊。"

"如果真是那样的话，"大公主说道，"我真心地希望你能成为世界上最英俊迷人的王子，我愿意尽我所能把我的美丽分享给你。"

大公主刚说完，小凤头里凯就在她眼中变成了世界上最英俊迷人的王子，这可是公主见过的最帅气、最亲切的人了。有人说，王子和公主之所以发生如此大的变化，并不是仙女的法力而是他们彼此之间的真爱。他们说，公主看到了里凯的坚韧、审慎，看到里凯具有的智慧、判断力等一切优秀的思维品质后，进行适当的反思，就再也看不见他畸形的身体和丑陋的外貌了；在她看来，里凯驼背弯腰就是壮汉的虎背熊腰；他走路一瘸一拐的样子有种羞怯的感觉，反而成了吸引她的地方。他们还说，他那双斜眼在她的眼里格外炯炯有神；斜向一边的目光简直就是狂热爱情的表现；总之，就连他那枣红的大鼻子在她眼中都显得有点威武雄壮。

不管如何，大公主立刻答应，只要里凯王子能征得她父王的同意，自己就马上嫁给王子。国王得知自己的女儿非常爱慕里凯王子，而里凯又是世界上最有智慧、最有见地的王子，就欣然接纳里凯当女婿。第二天上午他们就举行了婚礼，正是小凤头里凯所预期且按自己命令筹备已久的婚礼。

Riquet with the Tuft

There was, once upon a time, a queen who was brought to bed of a son, so hideously ugly that it was long disputed whether he had human form. A fairy, who was at his birth, affirmed, he would be very lovable for all that, since he should be endowed with an abundance of wit. She even added that it would be in his power, by virtue of a gift she had just then given him, to bestow on the person he most loved as much wit as he pleased. All this somewhat comforted the poor queen, who was under a grievous affliction for having brought into the world such an ugly brat. It is true that this child no sooner began to prattle, but he said a thousand pretty things, and that in all his actions there was something so taking that he charmed everybody. I forgot to tell you that he came into the world with a little tuft of hair upon his head, which made them call him Riquet with the Tuft, for Riquet was the family name.

Seven or eight years after this, the queen of a neighboring kingdom was delivered of two daughters at a birth. The first-born of these was beautiful beyond compare, whereat the queen was so very glad that those present were afraid that her excess of joy would do her harm. The same fairy, who had assisted at the birth of little Riquet with the Tuft, was here also; and, to moderate the queen's gladness, she declared that this little princess should have no wit at all, but be as stupid as she was pretty. This mortified the queen extremely, but some moments afterwards she had far greater sorrow; for, the second daughter she was delivered of, was very ugly.

"Do not afflict yourself so much, Madam," said the fairy, "your daughter shall have so great a portion of wit that her want of beauty will scarcely be perceived."

"God grant it," replied the queen, "but is there no way to make the eldest, who is so pretty, have some little wit?"

"I can do nothing for her, Madam, as to wit," answered the fairy, "but everything as to beauty; and as there is nothing but what I would do for your satisfaction, I give her a gift that she shall have the power to make handsome the person who shall best please her."

As these princesses grew up, their perfections grew up with them; all the public talk was of the beauty of the eldest, and the wit of the youngest. It is true also that their defects increased considerably with their age; the youngest visibly grew uglier and uglier, and the eldest became every day more and more stupid; she either made no answer at all to what was asked her, or said something very silly; she was with all this so unhandy that she could not place four pieces of china upon the mantelpiece, without breaking one of them, nor drink a glass of water without spilling half of it upon her clothes. Though beauty is a very great advantage in young people, yet here the youngest sister bore away the bell, almost always, in all companies from the eldest; people would indeed, go first to the beauty to look upon, and admire her, but turn aside soon after to the wit, to hear a thousand most entertaining and agreeable turns, and it was amazing to see, in less than a quarter of an hour's time, the eldest with not a soul with her and the whole company crowding about the youngest. The eldest, though she was unaccountably dull, could not but notice it, and would have given all her beauty to have half the wit of her sister. The queen, prudent as she was, could not help reproaching her several times, which had liked to have made this poor princess die for grief.

One day, as she retired into the wood to bewail her misfortune, she saw, coming to her, a little man, very disagreeable, but most magnificently dressed. This was the young prince Riquet with the Tuft who having fallen in love with her, by seeing her picture, many of which went all the world over, had left his father's kingdom, to have the pleasure of seeing and talking with her.

Overjoyed to find her thus all alone, he addressed himself to her with all imaginable politeness and respect. Having observed, after he had made her the ordinary compliments that she was extremely melancholy, he said to her, "I cannot comprehend, Madam, how a person so beautiful as you are, can be so sorrowful as you seem to be; for though I can boast of having seen infinite numbers of ladies exquisitely charming, I can say that I never beheld anyone whose beauty approaches yours."

"You are pleased to say so," answered the princess, and here she stopped.

"Beauty," replied Riquet with the Tuft, "is such a great advantage that it ought to take the place of all things; and since you possess this treasure, I see nothing that can possibly very much afflict you."

"I had far rather," cried the princess, "be as ugly as you are, and have wit, than have the beauty I possess, and be so stupid as I am."

"There is nothing, Madam," returned he, "shows more that we have wit, than to believe we have none; and it is the nature of that excellent quality that the more people have of it, the more they believe they want it."

"I do not know that," said the princess, "but I know very well that I am very senseless, and thence proceeds the vexation which almost kills me."

"If that be all, Madam, which troubles you, I can very easily put an end to your affliction."

"And how will you do that?" cried the princess.

"I have the power, Madam," replied Riquet with the Tuft, "to give to that person whom I shall love best, as much wit as can be had; and as you, Madam, are that very person, it will be your fault only, if you have not as great a share of it as anyone living, provided you will be pleased to marry me."

The princess remained quite astonished, and answered not a word.

"I see," replied Riquet with the Tuft, "that this proposal makes you very uneasy, and I do not wonder at it, but I will give you a whole year to consider of it."

The princess had so little wit, and, at the same time, so great a longing to have some that she imagined the end of that year would never be; therefore she accepted the proposal which was made to her. She had no sooner promised Riquet with the Tuft that she would marry him on that day twelvemonth than she found herself quite otherwise than she was before; she had an incredible facility of speaking whatever she pleased, after a polite, easy, and natural manner; she began that moment a very gallant conversation with Riquet with the Tuft, wherein she tattled at such a rate that Riquet with the Tuft believed he had given her more wit than he had reserved for himself.

When she returned to the palace, the whole court knew not what to think of such a sudden and extraordinary change; for they heard from her now as much sensible discourse, and as many infinitely witty turns, as they had stupid and silly impertinences before. The whole court was overjoyed at it beyond imagination; it pleased all but her younger sister; because having no longer the advantage of her in respect of wit, she appeared, in comparison of her, a very disagreeable, homely puss. The king governed himself by her advice, and would even sometimes hold a council in her apartment. The noise of this change spreading everywhere, all the young princes of the neighboring kingdoms strove all they could to gain her favor, and almost all of them asked her in marriage; but she found not one of them had wit enough for her, and she gave them all a hearing, but would not engage herself to any.

However, there came one so powerful, rich, witty and handsome that she could not help having a good inclination for him. Her father perceived it, and told her that she was her own mistress as to the choice of a husband, and that she might declare her intentions. As the more wit we have, the greater difficulty we find to make a firm resolution upon such affairs, this made her desire her father, after having thanked him, to give her time to consider of it.

She went accidentally to walk in the same wood where she met Riquet with the Tuft, to think, the more conveniently, what she ought to do. While she was walking in a profound meditation, she heard a confused noise under her feet, as it were of a great many people who went backwards and forwards, and were very busy. Having listened more attentively, she heard one say, "Bring me that pot"; another "Give me that kettle"; and a third, "Put some wood upon the fire."

The ground at the same time opened, and she seemingly saw under her feet, a great kitchen full of cooks, scullions, and all sorts of servants necessary for a magnificent entertainment. There came out of it a company of roasters, to the number of twenty, or thirty, who went to plant themselves in a fine alley of wood, about a very long table, with their larding pins in their hands, and skewers in their caps, who began to work, keeping time, to the tune of a very harmonious song.

The princess, all astonished at this sight, asked them who they worked for.

"For Prince Riquet with the Tuft," said the chief of them, "who is to be married tomorrow."

The princess was more surprised than ever, and recollecting that it was now that day twelvemonth on which she had promised to marry Riquet with the Tuft, she was like to sink into the ground.

What made her forget this was that, when she made this promise, she was very silly, and having obtained that vast stock of wit which the prince had bestowed on her, she had entirely forgot her stupidity. She continued walking, but had not taken thirty steps before Riquet with the Tuft presented himself to her, bravely and most magnificently dressed, like a prince who was going to be married.

"You see, Madam," said he, "I am very exact in keeping my word, and doubt not, in the least, but you are come hither to perform yours, and to make me, by giving me your hand, the happiest of men."

"I shall freely own to you," answered the princess, "that I have not yet taken any resolution on this affair, and believe I never shall take such a one as you desire."

"You astonish me, Madam," said Riquet with the Tuft.

"I believe it," said the princess, "and surely if I had to do with a clown, or a man of no wit, I should find myself very much at a loss. 'A princess always observes her word,' would he say to me, 'and you must marry me, since you promised to do so.' But as he whom I talk to is the man of the world who is master of the greatest sense and judgment, I am sure he will hear reason. You know that when I was but a fool, I could, notwithstanding, never come to a resolution to marry you; why will you have me, now I have so much judgment as you gave me, and which makes me a more difficult person than I was at that time, to come to such a resolution, which I could not then determine to agree to? If you sincerely thought to make me your wife, you have been greatly in the wrong to deprive me of my dull simplicity, and make me see things much more clearly than I did."

"If a man of no wit and sense," replied Riquet with the Tuft, "would be entitled, as you say, to reproach you for breach of your word, why will you not let me, Madam, do likewise in a matter wherein all the happiness of my life is concerned? Is it reasonable that persons of wit and sense should be in a worse condition than those who have none? Can you pretend this; you who have so great a share, and desired so earnestly to have it? But let us come to fact, if you please. Setting aside my ugliness and deformity, is there anything in me which displeases you? Are you dissatisfied with my birth, my wit, humor, or manners?"

"Not at all," answered the princess; "I love you and respect you in all that you mention." "If it be so," said Riquet with the Tuft, "I am like to be happy, since it is in your power to make me the most lovable of men."

"How can that be?" said the princess.

"It will come about," said Riquet with the Tuft, "if you love me enough to wish it to be so; and that you may no ways doubt, Madam, of what I say, know that the same fairy, who, on my birthday, gave me for gift the power of making the person who should please me extremely witty and judicious, has, in like manner, given you for gift the power of making him, whom you love, and would grant that favor to, extremely handsome."

"If it be so," said the princess, "I wish, with all my heart, that you may be the most lovable prince in the world, and I bestow it on you, as much as I am able."

The princess had no sooner pronounced these words, but Riquet with the Tuft appeared to her the finest prince upon earth; the handsomest and most amiable man she ever saw. Some affirm that it was not the enchantments of the fairy which worked this change, but that love alone caused the metamorphosis. They say that the princess, having made due reflection on the perseverance of her lover, his discretion, and all the good qualities of his mind, his wit and judgment, saw no longer the deformity of his body, nor the ugliness of his face; that his hump seemed to her no more than the homely air of one who has a broad back; and that whereas till then she saw him limp horribly, she found it nothing more than a certain sidling air, which charmed her. They say farther that his eyes, which were very squinting, seemed to her all the more bright and sparkling; that their irregularity passed in her judgment for a mark of a violent excess of love; and, in short, that his great red nose had, in her opinion, somewhat of the martial and heroic.

Howsoever it was, the princess promised immediately to marry him, on condition he obtained her father's consent. The king being acquainted that his daughter had an abundance of esteem for Riquet with the Tuft, whom he knew otherwise for a most sage and judicious prince, received him for his son-in-law with pleasure; and the next morning their nuptials were celebrated, as Riquet with the Tuft had foreseen, and according to the orders he had a long time before given.

小拇指

很久以前,一个樵夫和老婆生了七个儿子。老大也不过十岁,老小竟也已经七岁了。人们可能就要好奇了,樵夫如何能在这么短的时间生了这么多孩子呢。这是因为他的妻子会灵活生产,每胎都至少生两个。夫妻俩的生活本来就很拮据,现在再加上七个孩子,生活就更加苦不堪言了,因为七个孩子都还太小,根本不能自食其力。但更令夫妻二人烦恼的是,小儿子不仅十分瘦弱,而且总是沉默寡言。夫妻二人还以为小儿子是个傻子呢,但其实这正是他的精明之处。出生时,小儿子就非常瘦小,和小拇指一样小,所以人们都叫他"小拇指"。

小拇指这个可怜的孩子在家中尽受欺负,无论有没有做错事,最后都是他的错。然则,事实上他比任何一个哥哥都要精明,甚至这六个哥哥的智商加在一起都比不过他,因为他总是少说话,多听多思考。

恰逢这一年,年景不好,饥荒严重,穷人们为了保命,迫不得已只能舍弃孩子。一天晚上,孩子们都入睡了,樵夫挨着妻子坐在火堆旁,悲痛欲绝地对她说:"你很清楚,我们现在根本养不活孩子们了,但我又不忍心看见他们饿死在我的面前,所以我决定明天把他们都丢到森林里边。这事倒也不难,我们只要像往常一样把孩子带到森林里,趁他们在那儿忙着捆柴禾,不注意我们的时候赶紧偷偷遛掉就好了。"

"啊!"妻子嚷嚷起来,"你怎么能这么狠心故意抛弃自己的亲生骨肉呢?"

无论丈夫怎么向妻子解释目前他们太过贫穷，都无济于事，妻子怎么都不同意那样做。她虽然很穷，但她却是他们的亲生母亲啊。然而，妻子一想到，看着孩子们饿死在自己的面前又该是多么的痛心，最后还是同意了丈夫的决定，泪流满面地爬上床去。

父亲和母亲的对话，小拇指听得一清二楚。原来，躺在床上的小拇指注意到爸爸妈妈忙于商谈着什么，就悄悄地起床，躲到了父亲的板凳下面，以便在不暴露自己的情况下听清父母谈话。随后，他又回到床上，只是一整晚都没合眼，脑子里一直在想着自己该怎么办。第二天早上，小拇指早早地起床，来到河边捡了白色的小鹅卵石装满自己的口袋里，然后往家里走去。接下来，

在夫妻二人的带领下，一家人都出了门，不过小拇指并没有把自己昨晚听到的对话告诉哥哥们。此时，夫妻二人带着孩子们来到了一片茂密的森林，在这里人只要离开十步，就看不见人影了。开始，樵夫砍柴，孩子们就在那儿捡树枝，再捆起来。随后，夫妻二人趁孩子们忙活时，慢慢地退到丛林后，沿着一条小岔道一溜烟就逃走了。

当孩子们回过神来，发现爸爸妈妈不见了，开始嚎啕大哭。小拇指并没有把哥哥们的哭声放在心上，放任他们大哭，毕竟他非常清楚该如何重新回到家中，因为他早已在他们来时的路上撒下了放在口袋里的白色的小鹅卵石作为标记。然后，他就对哥哥们说："不用担心，哥哥们。爸爸妈妈把我们丢在了这儿，但是我可以带着你

们重新回到家中，你们只要跟着我走就好了。"哥哥们跟在小拇指的后面，穿过树林，原路返回。然而，他们不敢立马进家，而是躲在了家门口，想听爸爸妈妈正在说什么呢。

原来，樵夫和妻子回到家的时候，适逢庄园主送来十克朗金币——这钱是很久以前欠他的，夫妻俩早就不指望他还了。不过，这十金币可让他们又有了生路，毕竟他们可怜得快要饿死了。于是，樵夫立马让妻子去肉店，因为他们已经好久都没有吃上肉了。妻子从肉店买回来许多肉，足够他们俩吃三顿。饱餐后，妻子说道："唉！可怜的孩子，你们现在在哪儿呀？要是他们在这儿的话，也可以享享口福啊。当时就是你，威廉，非要把他们丢掉。我跟你说过，我们这么做一定会后悔的。也不知道他们现在在森林里怎么样了？唉！上帝啊，他们会不会已经被野狼吃掉了？你真是个没有心肝的家伙，竟然就这么把自己的亲生骨肉给抛弃了。"

妻子在这儿唠唠叨叨地说个不停，一直在重复着"自己是正确的，她早就说过他们会后悔的"，说了二十多遍。最后，樵夫被妻子唠叨得失去了耐心，大发脾气，并扬言妻子要是再说个不停，就要动手打她了。其实，樵夫内心一点都不比妻子好受，但是妻子真是太啰嗦了，毕竟他和大多数男人状态一样，都喜欢妻子的金玉良言，但又会对永远正确的妻子感到不耐烦，认为她们纠缠不休。妻子悲痛欲绝，泪流满面地哭喊着："唉！我可怜的孩子，你们现在……在哪儿呢？"

她呼唤时声音很大，连门外的孩子们都听见了，于是他们异口同声地哭喊道："在这儿，我们在这儿呢。"

听到孩子们的声音，妻子立马跑出去打开门，将孩子们一把揽入自己的怀中，说道："亲爱的孩子们，看见你们我真是太高兴了。你们一定饿了吧，累了吧？可怜的彼得，你看你身上脏的。快，快点进来，让我好好给你洗洗。"

看到这，你得知道，彼得是七个孩子里面最大的一个，同时也是妻子最喜欢的孩子，因为彼得长有橘红色的头发，而她自己也长有橘红色的头发。看着孩子们坐在餐桌前大口地吃着晚饭，夫妻二人很是欣慰。随后，孩子们几乎异口同声地向爸爸妈妈讲述，他们自己在森林里有多么可怕。夫妻二人看到一家人再次团聚，都非常高兴，只要这十克朗金币没有花完，一家人就可以一直这么幸福地生活下去。然而，等到金币花完时，夫妻俩再次陷入之前的窘境，所以决定再次把孩子们拐掉。而且可以确定的是，这一次他们俩可能会把孩子们带到更远的地方去。樵夫和妻子秘密商量着这件事儿，不料又被小拇指偶然听到了，于是他还是决定用老办法去摆脱困境。第二天清晨，小拇指准时起床，打算前往小河边捡一些小鹅卵石，但令他沮丧的是，门已经被爸爸妈妈上了两道锁，他只好站在那儿思考着到底该如何是好。看到父亲走之前给了他们每人一块面包作为早餐，他灵机一动，想着可以用面包屑代替鹅卵石，沿路做些标记，所以他就把面包装在了自己的口袋里。

爸爸妈妈把孩子们带到森林中植被最浓密、光线最弱的地方后，偷偷溜到一条小岔道上，就这样又把孩子们给抛弃了。小拇指并没有因此而感到惊慌失措，因为他认为自己可以轻轻松松地依据来时自己丢下的面包屑找到回家的路。但是令他吃惊的是，现在他根本就看不到面包屑了，因为这些面包屑早就被鸟儿吃光了。这下可苦了这些孩子们，他们走得越远，越迷路，在密林里越来越晕头转向。

夜幕降临，天空刮起了狂风，越刮越可怕。他们还设想听到四面八方都是狼的叫声，来把他们全都吃掉一般。孩子们一个个吓得既不敢出声，也不敢回头看。随后，又下起了瓢泼大雨，他们浑身都湿透了，加上地面湿滑，他们每走一步就会摔倒一次，爬起来时已经浑身污泥，就连双手都不知该往哪儿放了。

小拇指为了发现周边的情况，就爬到一棵树顶上，转着脑袋向四周眺望，最后看到森林远处闪烁着一束烛光般的微光。小拇指从树上爬下来，落地之后，就看不见那束微光了，这让他很是沮丧。但是幸运的是，他和哥哥们朝着刚刚在树上看到的亮光方向走去，走了一段时间，当他走出森林后，他才又一次看到了那束亮光。

最后，他们心惊胆战地朝着发出烛光的房屋走去，这一路走来，每次走到低洼处，他们就常常看不见亮光了。他们敲了敲门，只见前来开门的是一位善良的夫人，问他们有什么事。

小拇指告诉她，他们很可怜，在森林里迷路了，能否看在上帝的份上收留他们一晚上。夫人看到这么可爱的孩子，泪水夺眶而出，对他们说："唉，可怜的孩子，你们从哪儿来的？你们可知道这座房子的主人是一个残暴的食人魔，专吃小孩子呢？"

"唉，亲爱的夫人，那我们该怎么办呢？"小拇指（同哥哥们一样冻得瑟瑟发抖）问道，"如果你不收留我们的话，今晚森林里的狼肯定会吃掉我们的；要是那样的话，还不如让食人魔吃掉呢。食人魔或许还会可怜我们的，如果你能替我们向他求情的话。"

食人魔的妻子心想，自己可以瞒着丈夫先收留孩子们一夜，第二天一早就让他们离开。于是她就让孩子进了屋，并将他们带到火炉旁取暖。因为此时，烤肉杆上正放着一头全羊，那是给食人魔烤的，作为它的晚餐。

孩子们刚暖和一点，就听到门外传来三四声"砰、砰砰、砰砰砰"的捶门声，原来是食人魔回来了。一听到声音，食人魔的妻子就把孩子们藏到床底下，然后才去开门。回到家里，食人魔直接问晚饭做好了没有，酒倒上了没有，然后才坐在自己的位子上开始大吃起来。其实，羊肉没有烤熟，还夹带着血，不过这正合他的口味。突然间，他向左右嗅了嗅，说道："我闻到了鲜肉的味道。"

"你闻到的，"妻子说道，"一定是我刚杀的小牛，已经剥皮了。"

"我再说一遍，我闻到的可是鲜肉味。"食人魔盯着妻子，怒气冲冲，回应道，"肯定瞒着我，在这里一定藏了什么东西。"

他一边说着，一边从饭桌旁边站起来，径直走到了床边。

"唉！"他说道，"我就知道你会骗我，你这该死的女人。我怎么没有把你一起吃掉，你个老畜生。哈哈，这批野味来得正巧，过上一两天就有三个朋友要来拜访我，到时正好可以用来款待我的朋友。"

说完，他就把孩子们一个个地从床底下拽了出来。可怜的孩子们跪在食人魔面前，祈求他放过自己。然而，站在他们面前的可是世界上最残酷无情的食人魔，一点也不会同情他们，而且双眼充满杀意，仿佛要把他们吞食掉一般。他告诉妻子，准备一些上等的酱汁，把这些孩子做成美味佳肴。说着，食人魔拿起大刀，左手提着一块巨大的磨刀石，走到可怜的孩子们面前霍霍地磨起刀来。就在他抓起一个孩子准备动手时，妻子对他说："你现在急着做什么？明天再杀不是更好吗？"

"住嘴！"食人魔说道，"现在宰了，吃起来才更嫩呢。"

"但是，你还有那么多肉呢，"妻子回答道，"现在还有一头牛，两只羊，还有半头猪，全都没有吃呢。"

"说的也是，"食人魔说道，"先给他们吃饱肚子，可别让他们饿瘦了，然后再把他们放到床上睡觉去。"

好心的夫人听了喜出望外，给孩子们摆上了丰盛的晚餐，但是他们吓得心惊胆战，一点都吃不下。那个食人魔呢，再次坐到桌前喝起酒来。一想到自己有那么多美味佳肴款待自己的朋友，他开心得不得了，于是就比平时多喝了十几杯，最后喝得晕晕乎乎的，上床睡着了。

食人魔共有七个女儿，都是小孩子。这七个小食人魔和父亲一样都经常吃鲜肉，所以皮肤也都非常白皙细腻，但是全都长着圆溜溜的小灰眼、鹰钩鼻和大嘴巴，牙齿长得又尖又长，而且牙齿间的空隙很大。她们还不算残忍，可是她们正在朝着这个方向发展，毕竟她们也是咬过一些小孩，喝过人血了。七个小食人魔早早就上床休息了，每个人头上都戴着一顶金冠。在同一个房间里还有一张同样大的床，食人魔的妻子把七个小男孩放在这张床上之后，就回到丈夫那里睡觉去了。

小拇指看到食人魔的女儿们头上都戴着一顶金冠，又想到食人魔会不会醒来后悔没有杀了他们。小拇指越想越害怕，于是就半夜起床，轻轻地取下哥哥们的帽子和自己的帽子，在取下小食人魔的金冠后，将金冠戴在哥哥们和自己的头上，又把帽子戴在七个小食人魔头上。这样食人魔可能就会错把他们当成自己的女儿，而把女儿当作自己要杀的小男孩们。不出所料，食人魔半夜醒来果真后悔把当天要办的事儿推迟到第二天早上了，于是急匆匆地从床上跳下来，拿起他那把大刀。

"让我看看，"他说道，"如何处置这群小家伙们，不能再犹豫了。"

随后，他走上前，摸索着来到了女儿们的房间，走向小男孩的床边，床上除小拇指之外的所有男孩子都熟睡了。食人魔伸手挨个摸了摸孩子们的脑袋，摸到小拇指时，真是把小拇指吓得魂不附体。食人魔摸到金冠时，惊道："险些酿成大祸了，看来我昨晚真是喝多了。"

于是他又来到了女儿们的床边，摸到了男孩们的帽子。"哈哈，"他说道，"我的小家伙们，原来你们在这儿呀！开始动手吧！"

说完手起刀落，食人魔割断了全部七个女儿的喉咙。

食人魔对自己的这一举动非常满意，随后又回到了妻子身边继续睡觉。小拇指一听到食人魔的鼾声，就叫醒哥哥们，让他们立即穿上衣服，跟着自己走。然后，弟兄七个就悄悄地来到花园，翻墙逃了出去。就这样，他们浑身颤抖跑了几乎一整夜，也不清楚自己要跑到什么地方去。

食人魔醒来后，对妻子说："上楼去，把昨晚来这儿过夜的几个小家伙收拾收拾。"妻子听错了，以为丈夫是让她去给孩子们穿穿衣服呢，所以她对丈夫这一善良之举感到非常惊讶，她没有料到丈夫想以何种方式让她去收拾孩子们，转而心想既然丈夫都已经吩咐自己去给那几个男孩穿衣服，那还是去吧。然而，她惊骇地发现七个女儿被杀，正躺在血泊之中，她晕了过去，毕竟遇到这种事情所有女人几乎都会受不了打击而昏厥过去。食人魔担心给妻子安排的活儿要花很长时间，就亲自上楼来帮她。看到这惊悚的一幕，食人魔同样惊呆了。

"哎呀！是我干的吗？"他哭喊道，"这帮该死的混蛋，一定要找他们算账，我立马就去。"然后他往妻子脸上泼了一罐水，让她醒了过来。"快，快点，"他吼道，"拿来我的七里靴，我要去把他们都抓回来。"

食人魔奔出去，开始是向各个不同的方向跑了好一阵子，不过最后还是朝着男孩们逃跑的那条路追了过去。可怜的孩子们只要再跑一百多步就能安全到家了，可是却见食人魔轻而易举一步步翻过一座座大山，并像越过沟渠一般轻松地跨过一条条大河。此时，小拇指看到附近有一个岩洞，忙让哥哥们都躲到里面去，他自己也挤了进去，焦虑着食人魔会做什么。

食人魔瞎跑了许多冤枉路（穿七里靴走路又极其累人），就想要休息一下。但巧的是，他坐下来休息的岩石正是这些小男孩藏身的地方。食人魔太疲倦了，就睡着了，不一会儿开始发出鼾声。这鼾声是如此惊悚，吓得孩子们直打哆嗦，与食人魔提刀要割他们喉咙一样可怕。小拇指比较沉着勇敢，告诉哥哥们赶紧趁着食人魔酣睡时跑回家去，不用为他担心。哥哥们听了小拇指的建议，马上跑回家中。然后，小拇指走到食人魔身边，轻轻地脱下他的七里靴，穿在自己的脚上。本来七里靴又长又大，但七里靴可不是普通的靴子，它有魔力，能够根据穿靴人脚的大小做出调整，所以小拇指将靴子穿在脚上时就非常合适，仿佛是专门为他定制的。

小拇指很快来到了食人魔的家中，只见食人魔妻子正在为失去女儿而哭得伤心欲绝。"你的丈夫，"小拇指说道，"现在非常危险，被一群强盗抓住了。强盗们扬言要是他不交出所有金银珠宝的话，就要杀人灭口。就在强盗们把刀抵在他脖子上的时候，他看到了我，希望我能来，来告诉你他的遭遇，并说让你把所有有价值的东西全都拿出来交给我，一件都不留。否则，强盗们就会毫不留情地杀了他。由于当时情况非常紧急，他还让我穿上了他的七里靴（你看他的靴子就在我的脚上）。这样不仅能确保我尽快赶过来，同时还能证明我没有骗你。"

善良的夫人，伤心难过，害怕得要命，就把所有家当都给了小拇指，毕竟食人魔是一个好丈夫，尽管过去常常吃小孩。小拇指就这样拿到了食人魔所有的钱财，然后就赶回了家中，受到了全家人的热烈欢迎。

很多人并不同意这一情况，自认为小拇指压根儿没有盗窃食人魔的财物，相反却是非常正直，有良知，他只是脱掉食人魔的七里靴，穿在脚上跑去追自己的哥哥们罢了，并没有用它来做坏事。对此他们深信不疑，而且相信的人越来越多，毕竟他们经常在樵夫家又喝又吃的。他们斩钉截铁地说，小拇指脱掉食人魔的靴子后曾去过一趟皇宫，因为他得知朝廷非常担心离这儿二百里格之外的那支军队，以及战争能否取得胜利。他们还说，小拇指面见了国王，并声称只要国王需要，他可以在入夜之前就把前线军队的消息报告给他。于是国王向小拇指承诺，只要他能做到就赏赐他一大笔丰厚的财产。小拇指非常信守承诺，果真在天黑之前将消息报给了国王。正是这头一次远门差事，让小拇指名声大噪，他想要什么就能得到什么。国王为向军队传达命令，给了小拇指十分优厚的报酬。还有一些已婚妇女，托他帮忙给丈夫传送家书，所给的报酬少得都不值得他跑一趟，他也不屑于估算这种微薄报酬。小拇指做了一段时间的信使，积攒了大笔财富之后就回到父母家。家人们见其回来，重新团聚时别提有多喜悦啦。他让全家都很富裕。就这样，小拇指不仅让他们在世界上体面生活安顿下来，同时也赢得了国王的青睐。

Little Thumb

There was, once upon a time, a man and his wife, faggot-makers by trade, who had seven children, all boys. The eldest was but ten years old, and the youngest only seven. One might wonder how that the faggot-maker could have so many children in so little a time; but it was because his wife went nimbly about her business and never brought fewer than two at a birth. They were very poor, and their seven children incommoded them greatly, because not one of them was able to earn his bread. That which gave them yet more uneasiness was that the youngest was of a very puny constitution, and scarce ever spoke a word, which made them take that for stupidity which was a sign of good sense. He was very little, and, when born, no bigger than one's thumb; which made him called Little Thumb.

The poor child bore the blame for whatsoever was done amiss in the house, and guilty or not was always in the wrong; he was, notwithstanding, more cunning and had a far greater share of wisdom than all his brothers put together, and if he spoke little he heard and thought the more.

There happened now to come a very bad year, and the famine was so great that these poor people resolved to rid themselves of their children. One evening, when they were all in bed and the faggot-maker was sitting with his wife at the fire, he said to her, with his heart ready to burst with grief, "You see plainly that we are not able to keep our children, and I cannot see them starve to death before my face; I am resolved to lose them in the wood tomorrow, which may very easily be done; for while they are busy in tying up the faggots, we may run away, and leave them, without their taking any notice."

"Ah!" cried out his wife. "And can you yourself have the heart to take your children out along with you on purpose to lose them?"

In vain did her husband represent to her their extreme poverty; she would not consent to it; she was, indeed poor, but she was their mother. However, having considered what a grief it would be to her to see them perish with hunger, she at last consented and went to bed all in tears.

Little Thumb heard every word that had been spoken; for observing, as he lay in his bed, that they were talking very busily, he had got up softly and hid himself under his father's stool that he might hear what they said, without being seen. He went to bed again, but did not sleep a wink all the rest of the night, thinking on what he ought to do. He got up early in the morning, and went to the river side where he filled his pockets full of small white pebbles, and then returned home. They all went abroad, but Little Thumb never told his brothers one syllable of what he knew. They went into a very thick forest, where they could not see one another at ten paces distance. The faggot-maker began to cut wood, and the children to gather up sticks to make faggots. Their father and mother seeing them busy at their work, got from them by degrees, and then ran away from them all at once, along a by-way, through the winding bushes.

When the children saw they were left alone, they began to cry as loud as they could. Little Thumb let them cry on, knowing very well how to go home again; for as he came he had taken care to drop all along the way the little white pebbles he had in his pockets. Then said he to them, "Be not afraid, brothers, father and mother have left us here, but I will lead you home again, only follow me." They did so, and he brought them home by the very same way they came into the forest. They dared not to go in, but sat themselves down at the door, listening to what their father and mother were saying.

The very moment the faggot-maker and his wife got home, the lord of the manor sent them ten crowns, which he had owed them a long while, and which they never expected. This gave them a new life for the poor people were almost famished. The faggot-maker sent his wife immediately to the butcher's. As it was a long while since they had eaten a bit, she bought thrice as much meat as would sup two people. Having filled their bellies, the woman said, "Alas! Where are now our poor children? They would make a good feast of what we have left here; but then it was you, William, who had a mind to lose them; I told you we should repent of it: what are they now doing in the forest? Alas! Dear God, the wolves have, perhaps, already eaten them up: you are very inhuman thus to have lost your children."

The faggot-maker grew at last quite out of patience, for she repeated this above twenty times that they should repent of it, and she was in the right of it for so saying. He threatened to beat her, if she did not hold her tongue. It was not that the faggot-maker was not, perhaps, more vexed than his wife, but that she teased him, and that he was of the humor of a great many others who love wives who speak right, but think those very importunate who are always in the right. She was half drowned in tears, crying out, "Alas! Where are now my children, my poor children?"

She spoke this so very loud that the children who were at the door, began to cry out all together, "Here we are, here we are."

She ran immediately to open the door, and said, hugging them, "I am glad to see you, my dear children; you are very hungry and weary; and my poor Peter, you are horribly bemired; come in and let me clean you."

Now, you must know, that Peter was her eldest son whom she loved above all the rest, because he was somewhat carroty, as she herself was. They sat down to supper, and ate with such a good appetite as pleased both father and mother whom they acquainted how frightened they were in the forest; speaking almost always all together. The good folks were extremely glad to see their children once more at home, and this joy continued while the ten crowns lasted; but when the money was all gone, they fell again into their former uneasiness, and resolved to lose them again; and that they might be the surer of doing it, to carry them at a much greater distance than before. They could not talk of this so secretly, but they were overheard by Little Thumb who made account to get out of this difficulty as well as the former; but though he got up betimes in the morning, to go and pick up some little pebbles, he was disappointed, for he found the house-door double-locked, and was at a stand what to do. When their father had given each of them a piece of bread for their breakfast, he fancied he might make use of this bread instead of the pebbles, by throwing it in little bits all along the way they should pass; and so he put it up into his pocket.

Their father and mother brought them into the thickest and most obscure part of the forest; when, stealing away into a by-path, they there left them. Little Thumb was not very uneasy at it, for he thought he could easily find the way again, by means of his bread which he had scattered all along as he came. But he was very much surprised when he could not find so much as one crumb; the birds had come and eaten it up every bit. They were now in great affliction, for the farther they went, the more they were out of their way, and were more and more bewildered in the forest.

Night now came on, and there arose a terrible high wind, which made them dreadfully afraid. They fancied they heard on every side of them the howling of wolves coming to eat them up; they scarce dared to speak, or turn their heads. After this, it rained very hard, which wet them to the skin; their feet slipped at every step they took, and they fell into the mire, whence they got up in a very dirty pickle; their hands were in a sorry state.

Little Thumb climbed up to the top of a tree, to see if he could discover anything; and having turned his head about on every side, he saw at last a glimmering light, like that of a candle, but a long way from the forest. He came down, and, when upon the ground, he could see it no more, which grieved him sadly. However, having walked for some time with his brothers towards that side on which he had seen the light, he perceived it again as he came out of the wood.

They came at last to the house where this candle was, not without abundance of fear, for very often they lost sight of it, which happened every time they came into a bottom. They knocked at the door, and a good woman came and opened it; she asked them what they wished.

Little Thumb told her they were poor children who had been lost in the forest, and desired to lodge there for God's sake. The woman seeing them so very pretty, began to weep, and said to them, "Alas! Poor babies, where do you come? Do you know that this house belongs to a cruel ogre who eats up little children?"

"Ah! Dear Madam," answered Little Thumb (who trembled every joint of him, as well as his brothers)," what shall we do? To be sure, the wolves of the forest will devour us tonight, if you refuse us to lie here; and so, we would rather the gentleman should eat us. Perhaps he will take pity on us, especially if you please to beg it of him."

The ogre's wife, who believed she could conceal them from her husband till morning, let them come in, and brought them to warm themselves at a very good fire; for there was a whole sheep upon the spit roasting for the ogre's supper.

As they began to be a little warm, they heard three or four great raps at the door; this was the ogre, who was home. Upon this she hid them under the bed, and went to open the door. The ogre presently asked if supper was ready, and the wine drawn; and then he sat himself down to table. The sheep was as yet all raw and bloody; but he liked it the better for that. He sniffed about to the right and left, saying, "I smell fresh meat."

"What you smell so," said his wife, "must be the calf which I have just now killed and flayed."

"I smell fresh meat, I tell you once more," replied the ogre, looking crossly at his wife, "and there is something here which I do not understand."

As he spoke these words, he got up from the table, and went directly to the bed.

"Ah!" said he. "I see how you would cheat me, you cursed woman; I know not why I do not eat up you too; but it is well for you that you are a tough old carrion. Here is good game, which comes very luckily to entertain three ogres of my acquaintance who are to pay me a visit in a day or two."

With that he dragged them out from under the bed one by one. The poor children fell upon their knees, and begged his pardon; but they had to do with one of the most cruel ogres in the world, who, far from having any pity on them, had already devoured them with his eyes; he told his wife they would be delicate eating, when tossed up with good savory sauce. He then took a great knife, and coming up to these poor children, whetted it upon a great whet-stone which he held in his left hand. He had already taken hold of one of them, when his wife said to him,"What need you do it now? It is time enough tomorrow?"

"Hold your prattling," said the ogre, "they will eat the tenderer."

"But you have so much meat already," replied his wife, "you have no occasion. Here is a calf, two sheep, and half a hog."

"That is true," said the ogre, "give them their belly-full that they may not fall away, and put them to bed."

The good woman was overjoyed at this, and gave them a good supper; but they were so much afraid, they could not eat a bit. As for the ogre, he sat down again to drink, being highly pleased that he had got wherewithal to treat his friends. He drank a dozen glasses more than ordinary, which got up into his head, and obliged him to go to bed.

The ogre had seven daughters, all little children, and these young ogresses had all of them very fine complexions, because they used to eat fresh meat like their father; but they had little grey eyes, quite round, hooked noses, wide mouths, and very long sharp teeth standing at a good distance from each other. They were not as yet over and above mischievous; but they promised very fair for it, for they already bit little children that they might suck their blood. They had been put to bed early, with everyone a crown of gold upon her head. There was in the same chamber another bed of the like bigness, and it was into this bed the ogre's wife put the seven little boys; after which she went to bed to her husband.

Little Thumb, who had observed that the ogre's daughters had crowns of gold upon their heads, and was afraid lest the ogre should repent his not killing them, got up about midnight; and taking his brothers' bonnets and his own, went very softly, put them upon the heads of the seven little ogresses, after having taken off their crowns of gold, which he put upon his own head and his brothers', that the ogre might take them for his daughters, and his daughters for the little boys whom he wanted to kill. All this succeeded according to his desire, for the ogre waking about midnight, and sorry that he deferred doing that till morning which he might have done overnight, threw himself hastily out of bed, and taking his great knife.

"Let us see," said he, "how our little rogues do, and not make two jobs of the matter."

He then went up, groping all the way, into his daughters' chamber; and came to the bed where the little boys lay, who were every soul of them fast asleep except Little Thumb, who was terribly afraid when he found the ogre fumbling about his head, as he had done about his brothers'. The ogre, feeling the golden crowns, said, "I should have made a fine piece of work of it truly; I find I guzzled too much last night."

Then he went to the bed where the girls lay; and having found the boys' little bonnets: "Hah!" said he. "My merry lads, are you there? Let us to work!"

And saying these words, without more ado, he cut the throats of all his seven daughters.

Well pleased with what he had done, he went to bed again to his wife. So soon as Little Thumb heard the ogre snore, he waked his brothers, and bade them put on their clothes presently, and follow him. They stole down softly into the garden, and got over the wall. They kept running almost all night, trembling all the while, without knowing which way they went.

The ogre, when he waked, said to his wife, "Go up stairs and dress those young rascals who came here last night." The ogress was very much surprised at this goodness of her husband, not dreaming after what manner he intended she should dress them; but thinking that he had ordered her to go and put on their clothes, went up, and was strangely astonished when she perceived her seven daughters killed, and weltering in their blood. She fainted away, for this is the first expedient almost all women find in such-like cases. The ogre, fearing his wife would be too long in doing what he had ordered, went up himself to help her. He was no less amazed than his wife, at this frightful spectacle.

"Ah! What have I done?" cried he. "The cursed wretches shall pay for it, and that instantly." He threw then a pitcher of water upon his wife's face; and having brought her to herself. "Give me quickly," cried he, "my boots of seven leagues, that I may go and catch them."

He went out; and, having run over a vast deal of ground, both on this side and that, he came at last into the very road where the poor children were, and not above a hundred paces from their father's house. They espied the ogre, who went at one step from mountain to mountain, and over rivers as easily as the narrowest channels. Little Thumb, seeing a hollow rock near the place where they were, made his brothers hide themselves in it, and crowded into it himself, minding always what would become of the ogre.

The ogre, who found himself much tired with his long and fruitless journey (for these boots of seven leagues extremely fatigue the wearer), had a great mind to rest himself, and, by chance, went to sit down upon the rock where these little boys had hid themselves. As he was worn out, he fell asleep: and, after reposing himself some time he began to snore so frightfully that the poor children were no less afraid of him, than when he held up his great knife, and was going to cut their throats. Little Thumb was not so much frightened as his brothers, and told them that they should run away immediately towards home, while the ogre was asleep so soundly; and that they should not be anxious about him. They took his advice, and got home presently. Little Thumb came up to the ogre, pulled off his boots gently, and put them on upon his own legs. The boots were very long and large, but as they were fairies, they had the gift of becoming big and little, according to the legs of those who wore them, so that they fitted his feet and legs as well as if they had been made on purpose for him.

He went immediately to the ogre's house, where he saw his wife crying bitterly for the loss of her murdered daughters. "Your husband," said Little Thumb, "is in very great danger, being taken by a gang of thieves, who have sworn to kill him, if he does not give them all his gold and silver. Just when they held their daggers at his throat, he perceived me, and desired me to come and tell you the condition he is in, and that you should give me whatsoever he has of value, without retaining any one thing; for otherwise they will kill him without mercy; and, as his case is very pressing, he desired me to make use (you see I have them on) of his boots, that I might make the more haste, and to show you that I do not impose upon you."

The good woman, being sadly frightened, gave him all she had: for this ogre was a very good husband, though he used to eat up little children. Little Thumb, having thus got all the ogre's money, came home to his father's house, where he was received with an abundance of joy.

There are many people who do not agree in this circumstance, and pretend that Little Thumb never robbed the ogre at all, and that he only thought he might very justly, and with safe conscience take off his boots of seven leagues, because he made no other use of them, but to run after little children. These folks affirm, that they were very well assured of this, and the more, as having drank and eaten often at the faggot-maker's house. They aver that when Little Thumb had taken off the ogre's boots, he went to court, where he was informed that they were very anxious about a certain army, which was two hundred leagues off, and the success of a battle. He went, say they, to the king, and told him that if he desired it, he would bring him the news from the army before night. The king promised him a great sum of money upon that condition. Little Thumb was as good as his word, and returned that very same night with the news; and this first expedition causing him to be known, he got whatever he pleased, for the king paid him very well for carrying his orders to the army. There were some married women, too, who sent letters by him to their husbands, but they paid him so ill that it was not worth his while, and turned to such small account that he scorned ever to reckon what he got that way. After having, for some time, carried on the business of a messenger, and gained thereby great wealth, he went home to his father, where it was impossible to express the joy they were all in at his return. He made the whole family very well-to-do; and by that means settled them very handsomely in the world, and, in the mean time, rose high in the king's favor.

荒谬的愿望

很久以前，有一个贫穷的樵夫，觉得生活过得实在是太艰难了。的确，他一直都在为那微不足道的收入而辛勤劳作。他虽然年轻，婚姻幸福，但有时候真希望自己在地下长眠算了。

一天，他正工作着，又一次悲叹起自己的命运。

"有些人，"他说，"只要许下愿望，立马就会得到上帝的恩准，他们的每一个愿望都能实现；但是我祈祷任何东西都没什么用，因为上帝对我这种人的祈祷充耳不闻。"

刚说完，天空中传来一声巨大的雷响，天神朱庇特出现在他面前，顿时电闪雷鸣。我们这位可怜的樵夫吓得惊慌失措，跪倒在地上。

"主啊，"他说，"忘记我刚才说的傻话吧；您不用理会我的愿望，只要不打雷了就好！"

"不要害怕，"天神朱庇特回答，"我听到了你的抱怨，来到这里是要告诉你，你错怪我了。听着，我，身为这个世界上至高无上的天神，向你承诺满足三个让你愉快的愿望。无论这些愿望是什么，只要你说出来，我都满足你。好好想想到底什么能给你带来欢乐和成功，还有当你身处逆境的时候，不要急于求成，一定要在脑海中再三思考再做决定。"

天神说完这些，就抽身上了奥林匹斯山。至于我们这位樵夫，则愉快地捆起木柴，背上肩，回家了。人在心情愉悦时，似乎肩上的重担也变轻了，樵夫大步向前走去，脑海里都是一些愉快的想法。一时之间许多愿望涌上他的心头，但他还是决心征求一下自己妻子的意见。妻子虽然年轻，但颇有见地。

很快，他就来到了家中，放下柴火："范妮，看我，"他说道，"赶紧生火，把木板铺开，不要舍不得。现在我们发达了，范妮，永远发达了。现在我们只需要想清楚要许什么愿就好。"

于是，他把今天发生的事情都告诉了妻子。范妮头脑灵活、思维敏捷，随即想了许多发家致富的方法，不过她非常认同丈夫的决定，要谨慎行事。

"要是因为我们缺乏耐心而失去机会，那就真是太可惜了，"她说，"最好今天晚上好好商量一下，明天再许愿。"

"说得好，"哈利回答道，"再去把我们家最好的酒取来，让我们好好庆祝一下美好的际遇。"

范妮从柴火堆后面的仓库里拿出一瓶酒，樵夫非常享受现在的舒适，靠在椅子上，脚伸到壁炉旁，手里还端着个高脚杯。

"多么明亮的余火啊！"他说，"多么暖和的炉火啊！要是手边再有个黑布丁就好了。"

令妻子大为吃惊的是，丈夫刚说完这些话，她就看到，一个长长的黑色布丁从壁炉的角落里冒了出来，一路歪歪扭扭地向她飞了过来。开始，她并不知道是怎么回事，害怕地大叫一声，随后她才意识到之所以发生这种奇怪的事情，是因为刚才丈夫轻率而愚蠢地说出了一个愿望，随即又沮丧地叫喊起来。出于愤怒和失望，她转身对着丈夫破口大骂，用她能想到的所有骂人的话把可怜的丈夫骂了个遍。

"废物！"她对他骂道，"当你可以祈求一个王国，祈求黄金、珍珠、红宝石、钻石、贵族服饰和数不清的财富时，你要黑布丁做什么！"

"不对，不对！"丈夫回答道，"是我刚才太草率了，酿成了大错。我现在要谨慎了，下次一定会做得更好。"

"谁知道你又会做出什么蠢事？"他的妻子反驳道，"一次愚蠢，永远愚蠢！"她任由自己发泄恼怒和坏脾气，继续责骂直到丈夫也被激怒，希望他自己要是一个鳏夫就好了，几乎就要脱口而出第二个愿望。

"够了！泼妇，"最后，他大吼起来，"控制一下你那不受控的嘴巴吧！谁曾听过这样无礼的话！一定要给这个泼妇一点颜色看看，希望上帝能把布丁挂在她的鼻尖上！"

丈夫刚说出这些话，愿望马上就实现了，那长长的黑布丁就嫁接到怒不可遏的妻子的鼻子上。

我们的樵夫一看见自己所做的错事后，立马停了下来。范妮本来年轻貌美，长相出众，但说实话，鼻尖上的这个布丁并没有衬托出她的美丽。然而，它也有一个好处，会有效抑制她讲话，因为布丁正好挂在她的嘴巴前面。

因此，现在就只剩下一个愿望了，樵夫差不多下定决定要好好利用起来，不能再耽搁了。他希望在任何不幸降临之前，能够拥有自己的王国。就在他打算说出这个愿望时，突然想到另外一件事。

"确实没有比国王更伟大的人了。"他自言自语道，"但是必须和国王一起享受这份尊荣的王后该怎么办呢？她顶着一个黑布丁大长鼻，怎么能优雅地坐在我旁边的宝座上呢？"

在这种进退两难的窘境下，他决定把这事儿交给范妮，由她决定自己到底是愿意一直顶着这么一个可怕而又损容貌的东西做皇后，还是愿意把这个丑陋的附属物从匀称的鼻子上去掉，继续做一个农夫的妻子。

　　范妮很快就做出了决定：虽然她梦想得到权位，但对于女人而言，放在第一位的永远是快乐。为了实现这一伟大的愿望，其他一切都必须让步，范妮宁愿做个穿着粗毛衣的美丽女人，也不愿做一个相貌丑陋的皇后。

　　因此，我们的樵夫并没有改变自己的生活状态，既没有成为一名君主，也没有腰缠万贯。但是他非常感激，能用自己所剩的一次机会许愿，实现了一个微不足道的愿望，立即帮助妻子摆脱了"累赘"。

The Ridiculous Wishes

In days long past there lived a poor woodcutter who found life very hard. Indeed, it was his lot to toil for little guerdon, and although he was young and happily married there were moments when he wished himself dead and below ground.

One day while at his work he was again lamenting his fate.

"Some men," he said, "have only to make known their desires, and straightway these are granted, and their every wish fulfilled; but it has availed me little to wish for ought, for the gods are deaf to the prayers of such as I."

As he spoke these words there was a great noise of thunder, and Jupiter appeared before him wielding his mighty thunderbolts. Our poor man was stricken with fear and threw himself on the ground.

"My lord," he said, "forget my foolish speech; heed not my wishes, but cease your thundering!"

"Have no fear," answered Jupiter, "I have heard your complaint, and have come hither to show you how greatly you do wrong me. Hark! I, who am sovereign lord of this world, promise to grant in full the first three wishes which it will please you to utter, whatever these may be. Consider well what things can bring you joy and prosperity, and as your happiness is at stake, be not over-hasty, but revolve the matter in your mind."

Having thus spoken Jupiter withdrew himself and made his ascent to Olympus. As for our woodcutter, he blithely corded his faggot, and throwing it over his shoulder, made for his home. To one so light of heart the load also seemed light, and his thoughts were merry as he strode along. Many a wish came into his mind, but he was resolved to seek the advice of his wife who was a young woman of good understanding.

He had soon reached his cottage, and casting down his faggot: "Behold me, Fanny," he said. "Make up the fire and spread the board, and let there be no stint. We are wealthy, Fanny, wealthy for evermore; we have only to wish for whatsoever we may desire."

Thereupon he told her the story of what had befallen that day. Fanny, whose mind was quick and active, immediately conceived many plans for the advancement of their fortune, but she approved her husband's resolve to act with prudence and circumspection.

"'What a pity," she said, "to spoil our chances through impatience. We had best take counsel of the night, and wish no wishes until tomorrow."

"That is well-spoken," answered Harry. "Meanwhile fetch a bottle of our best, and we shall drink to our good fortune."

Fanny brought a bottle from the store behind the faggots, and our man enjoyed his ease, leaning back in his chair with his toes to the fire and his goblet in his hand.

"What fine glowing embers!" he said. "And what a fine toasting fire! I wish we had a black pudding at hand."

Hardly had he spoken these words when his wife beheld, to her great astonishment, a long black pudding which, issuing from a corner of the hearth, came winding and wriggling towards her. She uttered a cry of fear, and then again exclaimed in dismay, when she perceived that this strange occurrence was due to the wish which her husband had so rashly and foolishly spoken. Turning upon him, in her anger and disappointment she called the poor man all the abusive names that she could think of.

"What!" she said to him. "When you can call for a kingdom, for gold, pearls, rubies, diamonds, for princely garments and wealth untold, is this the time to set your mind upon black puddings!"

"Nay!" answered the man. "It was a thoughtless speech, and a sad mistake; but I shall now be on my guard, and shall do better next time."

"Who knows that you will?" returned his wife. "Once a witless fool, always a witless fool!" And giving free rein to her vexation and ill-temper she continued to upbraid her husband until his anger also was stirred, and he had well-nigh made a second bid and wished himself a widower.

"Enough! Woman," he cried at last, "put a check upon your froward tongue! Who ever heard such impertinence as this! A plague on the shrew and on her pudding! Would to heaven it hung at the end of her nose!"

No sooner had the husband given voice to these words than the wish was straightway granted, and the long coil of black pudding appeared grafted to the angry dame's nose.

Our man paused when he beheld what he had wrought. Fanny was a comely young woman, and blest with good looks, and truth to tell, this new ornament did not set off her beauty. Yet it offered one advantage that as it hung right before her mouth, it would thus effectively curb her speech.

So, having now but one wish left, he had all but resolved to make good use of it without further delay, and, before any other mischance could befall, to wish himself a kingdom of his own. He was about to speak the word, when he was stayed by a sudden thought.

"It is true," he said to himself, "that there is none so great as a king, but what of the queen that must share his dignity? With what grace would she sit beside me on the throne with a yard of black pudding for a nose?"

In this dilemma he resolved to put the case to Fanny, and to leave her to decide whether she would rather be a queen, with this most horrible appendage marring her good looks, or remain a peasant wife, but with her shapely nose relieved of this untoward addition.

Fanny's mind was soon made up: although she had dreamt of a crown and scepter, yet a woman's first wish is always to please. To this great desire all else must yield, and Fanny would rather be fair in drugget than be a queen with an ugly face.

Thus our woodcutter did not change his state, did not become a potentate, nor fill his purse with golden crowns. He was thankful enough to use his remaining wish to a more humble purpose, and forthwith relieved his wife of her encumbrance.